# The Devil in Whitechapel

## *The Untold Story of Jack the Ripper*

# Robert Keller

**Please Leave Your Review of This Book At**
**http://bit.ly/kellerbooks**

ISBN-13:978-1536907964

ISBN-10:1536907960

© 2016 by Robert Keller

robertkellerauthor.com

# Table of Contents

# Part 1:
# The Whitechapel Murders

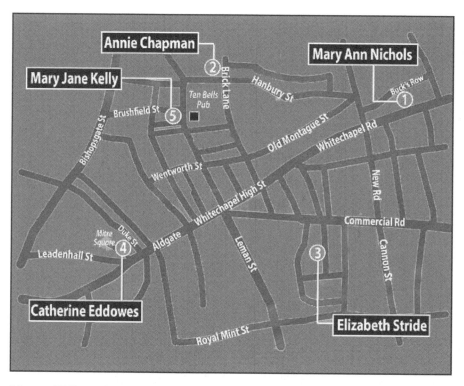

*Map of Whitechapel and Spitalfields, showing the locations of the five "Canonical Murders" attributed to Jack the Ripper*

# The Devil in Whitechapel

During the autumn of 1888, a series of murders occurred in London's East End that sent shockwaves reverberating around the world. The victims were all prostitutes, their killer, a knife-wielding assailant with an insatiable bloodlust. Within the space of just three months, this unnamed fiend would claim at least five lives. Then, he mysteriously vanished, leaving behind a trail of mutilated corpses and a scar upon our collective psyche that endures to this day.

Contrary to popular belief, Jack the Ripper was not the world's first serial killer. Who it is that holds that dubious distinction is unknown, although there are documented cases of serial murder going back to the Roman Empire and to China's Han Dynasty. Further along the historical path, we can point to Gilles de Rais, a 15th-century French nobleman accused of murdering over 140 children, or to Peter Stumpp, an alleged werewolf who terrorized the German town of Bedburg, a hundred years later. Among the Ripper's contemporaries, we find any number of psychopathic killers, including serial poisoner Mary Ann Cotton, depraved nurse Jane Toppan, and Chicago's notorious "Torture Doctor" Dr. H.H. Holmes.

So Jack wasn't the first. It would be safe to say, though, that no serial killer in history has garnered as much morbid attention as the Whitechapel murderer. Indeed, there can be few historical figures who have had as many manuscripts dedicated to them, from quasi-fiction potboilers to scholarly works of doctoral quality. In addition, there have been films, TV specials, plays, comic books, themed walks, even an opera. More recently, there have been internet sites and chatrooms where Ripper aficionados can debate their pet theories to their hearts' content.

Why our obsession with this one case?

Perhaps it's because it is the classic murder mystery. A fiend emerges from the fog, taking victims at will, his bloodlust escalating with each crime. Then, after a finale of unspeakable violence, he vanishes, leaving us to ponder who he was, why he did what he did, and why he suddenly stopped. It has all the elements of a perfect whodunit, except that there is no Sherlock Holmes or Hercule Poirot to point out the killer for us.

Will we ever know Jack's identity? Sadly, the answer to that question is, probably not. Many a name has been put forward but none of them entirely fits the bill.

But that is not to say that we know nothing about the Ripper. We have a good idea, via the testimony of eyewitnesses, as to what he looked like; we are able, through an examination of the crimes, to form a strong picture of how and where he lived; criminal psychologists are able to enlighten us as to his motives and personality; the pathology reports give us insights into his modus operandi and address the important question of whether or not he had medical training.

So, in spite of the shroud of mystery that envelopes the case, we know quite a lot about Jack the Ripper. We just are not able to name him.

That, of course, hasn't stopped us trying. Countless authors have attempted, over the years, to convince us that they have uncovered the Ripper's true identity. In the main, the theories they have presented are dubious at best and often quite ridiculous. The Ripper was a homicidal cotton merchant, he was a famous painter, he was the heir to the British throne. Unfortunately, none of these are true. Rather they are the product of twisting the facts and dredging up questionable "evidence" in order to buffer a pet theory. That is not the approach that I will be taking in this book.

Instead, I'll be revisiting the crimes, scrutinizing the credentials of oft-mentioned suspects, and debunking the common myths surrounding the case. I'll be re-examining the evidence, calling on the help of some expert profilers, and finally constructing a picture of the most enigmatic killer in history. If that sounds like something that might interest you, then I welcome you along on an exploration of one of the world's great mysteries.

First, though, we'll need to walk in the footsteps of the Ripper. Permit me, if you will, to take you on a terrifying journey of the mind, back to London's East End on a cold and drizzly eve in August 1888.

# Murder Most Foul

## *The Unquiet Death of Mary Ann Nichols*

Polly Nicholls was drunk. That was not unusual, of course. Polly, like most of the estimated 1,200 prostitutes working in London's East End, had little else in life besides her regular tipple of cheap gin. Whoring was a tough business in the Whitechapel slums, exposing its practitioners to the risk of violence and disease for the pittance of three pence a time. Three pence, as it turned out, was also the price of a shot of gin and cash did not usually sit long in Polly's pockets before it was handed over to the publican at her local tavern.

On the cold drizzly evening of Thursday, August 30, 1888, Polly had followed her usual pattern, drinking away her profits as fast as she earned them. At around 12:30 a.m. on Friday, August 31, she staggered away from the Frying Pan Pub on Brick Lane and headed towards her lodging house at 18 Thrawl Street. A single bed for the night ran to four pence but Polly hadn't bothered to hold back any money. Attempts at haggling with the boarding house deputy also failed and Polly was duly ejected at around 1:40 a.m.

Not that it appeared to bother her unduly. Flushed with gin and in a jovial mood, she informed the deputy that she would be back and asked him to save a bed for her. "I'll soon have my doss money," she said, performing a jaunty little pirouette. "See what a jolly bonnet I've got." And with that, she was out the door and into the night.

It had rained intermittently that day, and as Polly left the boarding house a steady drizzle was falling. At the nearby Shadwell Dry Dock, a fire was raging out of control, casting an eerie reddish glow across the low hanging cloud, a portent perhaps of what was to come.

At around 2:30, Polly encountered a friend, Emily Holland, on Whitechapel Road. Emily offered her a bed for the night but Polly refused, saying that she would pay her own way. "I've had my doss money three times today and spent it," she said. "It won't be long before I'm back." Then she staggered off, heading East. It was the last time that anyone, bar her killer, saw Polly alive.

At around four o'clock that morning, a man named Charles Cross was walking along Buck's Row when he spotted something on the ground. It looked to him like a discarded tarpaulin, but as he drew closer, he realized that it was a woman, lying on her back, her skirts lifted up to her waist. Thinking that she was either drunk or the victim of an assault, Cross summoned help from another passerby, Robert Paul. Together they went to the woman's assistance.

The men approached the body cautiously, Cross dropping into a crouch to feel for a pulse. The woman's hands were limp and very cold. "I believe she's dead," he told his companion. Paul then carried out his own assessment, placing his ear to the woman's chest. "I think she's breathing," he said, "But only just."

The men then pulled down the woman's skirts out of propriety and trotted off in search of a policeman. In the gloom of the street, illuminated only by a single gas lamp some distance off, neither of them had noticed the horrendous wounds to Polly Nichols' throat, cuts so severe that they had almost decapitated her.

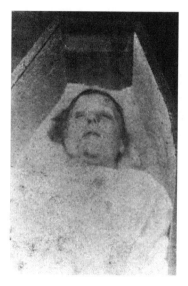

*Mary Ann Nichols*

A short while later, Cross and Paul encountered PC Mizen on Old Hanbury Street and told him what they had found. Mizen immediately set off towards Buck's Row. By the time he arrived, another policeman, Constable John Neil, had discovered the body. Using his lantern, Neil surveyed the gruesome scene. The woman's eyes were open, and blood was oozing from the wounds to her throat. Neil was baffled, though, as to why there wasn't more of it. With cuts like that, the scene should have been drenched in the stuff. And there was another peculiar detail. Although, the corpse's hands and lower arms were ice cold, the upper arms were still warm. Polly had not been dead long. Most likely, Cross and Paul had just missed catching her killer in the act.

Another constable, PC Thain, now arrived at the site and Neil sent him right away to fetch a local doctor, Dr. Llewellyn. Mizen, meanwhile, was sent to summon backup from the nearby Bethnal Green Police Station. When another officer, Sgt. Kirby arrived, he and Neil began knocking on doors, stirring sleepy residents from their slumber. No one, however, had seen or heard anything. It was as though Polly Nichols had been murdered by a ghost.

Dr. Rees Llewellyn arrived at the scene at shortly before four o'clock. He quickly examined the woman, estimating that she'd been dead no longer than half an hour. Cause of death was two deep slashes to the throat, running all the way round to the spinal column. The cuts ran so deep that they had severed the windpipe and esophagus.

By now, a crowd of early morning commuters had begun to gather, pushing forward for a glimpse at the gruesome scene. Dr. Llewellyn, therefore, suggested that the body be removed to the mortuary on Old Montague Street. He had, in any case, concluded his examination. Or so he thought.

Officers Neil, Mizen, and Kirby accompanied the corpse on the short ride to the morgue. PC Thain remained on site to await the arrival of Inspector John Spratling. When the inspector arrived, he discovered that the crime scene had been cleaned up, the blood washed away by a neighborhood boy. A quick survey of the area convinced him that there was nothing of import to be found there, so he headed for the mortuary to inspect the corpse himself. There, he lifted the woman's skirt and made a stunning discovery that had somehow been missed by the doctor and the other officers. Not only had Polly's throat been cut, but the killer had also ripped open her abdomen. A jagged cut ran from breastbone nearly to the pubic bone, the wound so deep that it left the woman's intestines exposed. A short while later the phone at Dr. Llewellyn's house jangled into life and he was summoned to the mortuary.

The second examination determined that the abdominal wound had been inflicted postmortem. It also cleared up the mystery of the lack of blood. There was bruising to the jaw and neck, including circular contusions to either side of the throat that appeared to be thumb imprints. This suggested that the woman had been throttled into submission before being cut. Perhaps, she'd even been strangled to death. That would explain why there'd been no spurt of blood from the carotid artery or jugular vein. Dr. Llewellyn also believed that she'd been lying down at the time the knife wounds were inflicted, causing blood to run down her neck and pool under her, much of it absorbed by her layers of clothing. Finally, the doctor revealed that the cuts had been inflicted by a left-handed person. (He'd later revise that opinion. Nonetheless, the myth of a left-handed Jack the Ripper endures to this day.)

Based on the autopsy report, the police were able to develop a theory about how the murder had occurred. They believed that the killer had strangled the woman with his hands, either killing her or rendering her unconscious. He then laid her on the ground before slashing her twice across the throat, inflicting wounds so deep that his blade notched the victim's spinal column. His bloodlust still not sated, he lifted the woman's skirt and ripped open her abdomen. His intention may well have been to inflict further atrocities but he'd been disturbed by the arrival of Charles Cross and had fled.

The next job for investigators was to identify the dead woman, no easy task when all she had in her possession was a comb, a broken mirror, and a handkerchief. However, as word of the murder spread across Whitechapel, the police heard of a woman named "Polly," who was missing from her lodgings at 18 Thrawl Street. "Polly" turned out to be Mary Ann Nichols, age 42. Her father and her husband identified her the next day.

Polly had been married to William Nichols, a printer's machinist by whom she had five children. But their marriage had broken down due to her drinking and she'd drifted into prostitution, selling herself on the streets for a pittance that was soon spent on booze in the nearest tavern. It was a pitiful life, brought to a brutal end.

The investigation into the murder of Polly Nicholls was assigned to Inspector Joseph Helson, head of CID for the J or Bethnal Green Division, in whose jurisdiction the body had been found. Helson immediately got to work, dispatching officers to search the streets and nearby stretches of rail line. They were looking for a weapon or perhaps a blood trail that might indicate which way the killer had fled. The search was extensive but in the end turned up nothing.

The other avenue of inquiry had officers knocking on doors, questioning the locals. But despite the fact that Polly Nicholls had been killed just feet away from several crowded residences, no one had seen or heard anything, not a scream, not the sound of a scuffle, nothing.

*Buck's Row, site of the Nichols Murder*

# Abberline Takes Charge

While all of these investigative efforts were ongoing, another, equally important, development was playing out. Scotland Yard had decided to get involved in the inquiry, bringing in their own man to oversee the efforts of the various divisional commanders on the ground. He was Chief Inspector Frederick George Abberline, a man whose name would become inextricably linked to the case. No other officer would develop a deeper knowledge of the Whitechapel murders. Indeed, other than Jack himself, Abberline is the personage most closely associated with the case.

*Chief Inspector Frederick Abberline*

At the time of the Ripper investigation, Abberline was a 25-year veteran of the force, with 14 of those years spent in the Whitechapel area. He was 45 years old, overweight and balding, his face decorated by a bushy mustache and equally bushy side whiskers. Abberline was an excellent investigator, with a stellar arrest record. Widely admired by his colleagues and superiors, Abberline was also well-loved by the community he served. On his transfer from Whitechapel to Scotland Yard, he'd been presented with a gold watch, inscribed with the message: "Presented, along with a purse of gold, to Inspector F.G. Abberline by the citizens of Whitechapel, Spitalfields etc., on his leaving the district after fourteen years' service, as a mark of his esteem and regard."

Why, you might ask, had the Metropolitan Police assigned such a senior officer to a simple prostitute murder? The reason may be because Polly Nicholls was not the only prostitute who had been brutally slain in the East End in recent times. Despite the hardship and random violence that were a fact of ghetto life, murder was a relatively rare occurrence. Yet, Polly's murder brought to three the number of unsolved homicides perpetrated against streetwalkers.

On the Bank Holiday Monday of August 6, 1888, Martha Tabram, a sturdily build prostitute in her late thirties, had been soliciting for trade on Whitechapel Road, in the company of another streetwalker, Mary Ann Connolly, known locally as "Pearly Poll."

They eventually hooked up with a couple of guardsmen, a corporal and a private, and spent some time drinking with them in various pubs along Whitechapel Road. At around 11:30, they paired up, Martha disappearing with one soldier into the darkened thoroughfare known as George Yard, while Pearly Poll led the other to another location close by.

Martha had often used George Yard for quick sex liaisons known colloquially as "four-penny knee tremblers." Usually, she favored the privacy of a tenement apartment block known as George Yard Buildings, where the staircase lights were usually turned off at 11 p.m., throwing the landings into pitch darkness. This was where she led the soldier.

In the early hours of that morning, Joseph and Elizabeth Mahoney returned to George Yard buildings having celebrated the Bank Holiday with friends. Afterward, Elizabeth went out again, to buy some supper at a chandler's shop on nearby Thrawl Street. She saw nothing untoward, neither while descending nor ascending the darkened staircase.

At around half past three in the morning Alfred George Crow, a cab-driver, returned home from work. While climbing the stairs, he spotted someone lying on the first-floor landing but paid scant attention. It was not unusual to find vagrants sleeping on the landings.

A little after 5 a.m., dock worker John Saunders Reeves left his home in George Yard Buildings on his way to work. He too saw the body lying on the ground, but by now it was getting light and Reeves could clearly see what Crow had missed, the pool of blood spreading out around the prone form. Reeves ran immediately to find a policeman and soon encountered Constable T. Barrett in George Yard.

It did not take long for Barrett to establish that the woman was dead. He then kept watch over the corpse while dispatching Reeves to the nearby home of Dr. Killeen. It took the doctor only a brief examination to pronounced the woman dead, in his opinion, brutally murdered. Killeen's later testimony at the inquest would quantify the savagery of the attack. The victim had suffered 39 knife wounds, most inflicted with an ordinary clasp knife but at least one caused by a long-bladed instrument, possibly a bayonet.

The investigation of the crime, described by deputy coroner George Collier as, "one of the most dreadful murders anyone could imagine," originally centered on the soldiers seen in Martha's company on the night she died. But that lead soon petered out and the case remained unsolved.

The other unsolved prostitute murder had occurred some months earlier, on April 2, 1888. In the early morning hours of that day, 45-year-old Emma Smith was savagely attacked by a gang of three men at the junction of Osborn and Wentworth Streets, just 100 yards from where Martha Tabram's body would be found. Emma was subjected to a vicious beating and then raped before a blunt object, possibly a stick, was forced into her vagina. The men then robbed her of the few pennies in her pockets before fleeing.

Emma Smith survived the initial attack, even managing to stagger back to her lodging house where several of the residents persuaded her to seek treatment at the London Hospital on Whitechapel Road. There, she told the doctors attending her what had happened. Unfortunately, her injuries were so severe that she succumbed to them the next day. It was not until April 6 that the police were informed of the murder. An inquest would later return a verdict of "Wilful murder against some person or persons unknown."

Many residents of Whitechapel believed that the attacks on Tabram and Smith were the work of the same man who had killed Polly Nichols. In the case of Emma Smith, this is quite obviously not the case. Smith was attacked by a group of men, and the motive appears to have been rape and robbery. Moreover, despite the brutality of the attack, it appears that the attackers did not intend murder. The men, according to Smith, had been drunk. It is quite likely that they simply took their assault too far.

But what of Martha Tabram? Is it possible that she fell victim to the same killer as Polly Nichols? On the face of it, the murders appear decidedly different. Martha was stabbed numerous times but not otherwise mutilated. Polly wasn't stabbed but had her throat cut and also suffered postmortem injuries. However, such a progression in modus operandi is not unheard of in serial murder cases. With the first murder the killer is still finding his way, so to speak. With the second he's more confident, able to inflict the injuries he has been fantasizing about for so long. It is entirely possible that Martha Tabram was Jack the Ripper's first victim. Ripper experts are split on the issue.

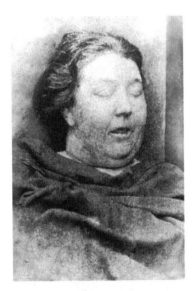

*Martha Tabram*

# The Man in the Leather Apron

In order to understand the Whitechapel murders, it is necessary to know something about the background against which they took place. A common misconception about this era is that the entire East End was one vast, teeming slum, inhabited by an immoral and criminal underclass one step removed from savages. This is simply not true. The area was impoverished, to be sure, but in the main it was well run and populated by decent, honest, and hardworking people. It was certainly no worse than slums in other, more salubrious London neighborhoods, like Chelsea, Westminster, and even the City itself.

Having said that, there were enclaves within the East End where the stereotype did run true, and one of those was the square mile in which the Ripper murders occurred. This was an area where thousands of people were crammed into crumbling tenements, a place where sheep and cattle were herded through the narrow streets to the many slaughterhouses, where the thoroughfares were littered with blood and excrement and the air was thick with the stench of rotting garbage, liquid sewage and the reek of the abattoirs. Most of the inhabitants lived under terrible conditions, many in lodging houses that charged between two and four pence per night. Four pence bought you a bunk. For two pence you could sleep standing up, crammed into a room with dozens of others, with ropes strung from wall to wall to prevent you falling over. More than half of the children born into this squalor died before

the age of five. Of those who survived, many were physically or
mentally handicapped.

For the most part, the people living in the East End during this era
were employed at menial work, although many were unemployed
and many more subsisted through various criminal enterprises.
For the East End's women, there was even less opportunity.
Prostitution was one of the few reliable means by which they
could earn a living. Police estimates put Whitechapel's prostitute
population in 1888, at 1,200. That is aside from those women who
took to occasional whoring to supplement their meager earnings.

In short, this was an area known for poverty and crime, squalor
and crowded tenements, narrow darkened thoroughfares, and
alleyways, where desperate women were forced out onto the
streets at night to make a living. The perfect hunting ground, in
other words, for an enterprising serial killer.

And yet, even in these conditions, murder was still a rarity. The
savage slaying of Polly Nichols caused great concern, especially as
most locals believed that the Tabram, Smith, and Nichols murders
had been committed by the same man. And this fear was fanned by
the press who alternately ran stories naming a criminal gang that
was preying on prostitutes, or a homicidal maniac stalking the
streets in search of prey. Many of these stories were later exposed
as fictions, but that did nothing to calm the growing panic. The
murders were by far the main topic of discussion in Whitechapel,
with women shuddering at the thought of the knife-wielding fiend
that might be lying in wait for them around the next corner. The
site where Polly Nichols had fallen became a sort of shrine,
attracting hordes of morbid curiosity seekers who did nothing but

stand around whispering in reverent tones while those who claimed to know pointed out the spot where the body had lain.

On the day of Polly's funeral, September 6, 1888, a huge crowd gathered in front of the morgue on Old Montague Street, and police officers had to be called in to clear a path so that the hearse could leave the premises. Crowds lined the streets as the procession made its way to the City of London Cemetery in Ilford, where Polly would be laid to rest. It was as though the entire community was united in grief.

In the meantime, a local merchant had sent a letter to the Home Secretary, Henry Matthews, urging him to offer a reward for the apprehension of the killer. Matthews refused, saying that it was not government policy to do so and reiterating his faith in the Metropolitan Police's ability to catch the criminal.

That belief appeared to be vindicated just days after the Nicholls murder, when detectives identified a suspect, a Polish Jew named John Pizer. Pizer was known locally as "Leather Apron," and made a habit of extorting money from prostitutes, beating them if they refused to pay. He was described as being five-foot-four, heavyset with a particularly thick neck. His eyes were "small and glistening," his lips perpetually parted in a menacing grin, his hair black and closely cropped. He wore a small, black moustache and was always attired in a black, leather apron, hence his nickname.

Leather Apron had once worked as a slipper maker but had apparently abandoned that trade for the easier pickings to be obtained by extortion. His M.O. was simplicity itself. Usually, he'd lurk outside taverns in the early morning hours, waiting for some tipsy prostitute to emerge alone. Then he'd follow the woman to a darkened stretch of road where he'd sneak up behind her, grab her by the throat and threaten violence unless she handed over her take. His victims said that he moved with incredible stealth. He was also said to carry a razor-sharp leather knife strapped to his waist, a remnant of his former vocation.

All of this made "Leather Apron" a very viable suspect in the Whitechapel murders. But finding him proved a difficult matter. And it was made even more problematic when the papers got wind of the story and started running articles which all but named Pizer as the Whitechapel killer. Fearful of mob justice, the suspect went into hiding with relatives. He was still at large when the Ripper claimed another victim.

# Lightning Strikes Again

## *The Murder of Dark Annie Chapman*

Annie Chapman had once been a respectable, married woman with three children. However, after her eldest died of meningitis at the age of just 12, both she and her husband, John, took to drink, leading to the eventual breakdown of their marriage. Things got even worse when John died and Annie lost the small allowance that he had provided her. Suffering from depression and alcoholism, and left with no means of support, she drifted into prostitution. At the age of 47, she was still working the streets, a sad and broken woman, living a life that teetered on the very edge of extinction.

Even among the generally unattractive streetwalkers of the East End, Annie was certainly no looker. Standing at just over five feet in height, she was stoutly built with dark hair, a pallid complexion, startling blue eyes and a thick nose. Her upper front teeth were missing. But for all her unattractiveness, she appears to have been a sweet soul, well-liked by everyone and a hard worker when she wasn't on the booze. Prostitution was not her only source of income, as she also did crochet work and made artificial flowers which she sold at a market stall in Stratford.

One of Annie's regular clients was a man named Ted Staley, who would often spend weekends with her. Known to her fellow lodgers as "the Pensioner," Staley appeared to be quite possessive over Annie and had once told her lodging house deputy not to allow her to bring any other men to the house. He was also the cause of the only altercation anyone ever saw her involved in.

The argument was over a bar of soap that Annie had borrowed from another lodger, Eliza Cooper, for Staley. When Annie failed to return the bar timeously, she and Cooper had words. A few days later, Annie appeared sporting several bruises, including a black eye.

While the injuries appeared fairly superficial, the same could not be said for

Annie Chapman's demeanor. Over the last few days of her life, she appeared listless and in obvious pain. Three days before she died she told a friend, Amelia Parker, that she was thinking of going to the hospital for treatment. She also confided that she didn't have money for food since she had been unable to work. Parker then gave her two pence to buy something to eat, warning her not to spend the money on booze. When she saw her again on September 7, Annie still looked poorly but in slightly better spirits. "It's no use giving way," she said. "I must pull myself together and get some money or I shall have no lodgings." These were the last words Annie Chapman ever spoke to her friend, Amelia.

At around 7 o'clock on that evening, Annie turned up at her lodging house at 35 Dorset Street and asked the deputy, Timothy Donovan, if she could sit in the kitchen. She remained there until around midnight when Donovan sent the night watchman, John Evans, to ask her for the money for her bed. Annie said that she didn't have any money as she had spent the last few days in the infirmary. She then went up to the office and tried to persuade

Donovan to let her stay the night. But it was clear to Donovan that she had been drinking and although he was fond of Annie, he refused. "If you can find money for beer, you can find money for your bed," he said.

Annie must have realized that arguing the point any further was futile. She turned to leave, admonishing Donovan to keep a bed for her. "I shall not be long before I am in," she said as she headed for the door, with John Evans in close attendance. He watched her as she tottered off towards Little Paternoster Row and turned right into Brushfield Street. "She was slightly tipsy," he'd later tell investigators, "but certainly not drunk."

Over the next three hours, we lose track of Dark Annie's whereabouts. One witness report had her in the Ten Bells Pub until 5 a.m., when she is said to have left with a man wearing a "little skull cap." This sighting has never been verified. What we do know is that by 5:30 a.m. Annie was on Hanbury Street in Spitalfields, just a short walk from the Ten Bells.

Hanbury Street was lined on either side by foreboding four-story buildings, each of which had been split into tiny residential units that were let to individuals or even to entire families. The front doors of these houses opened onto narrow passageways that ran the length of the building, past the staircase leading to the upper floors, all the way to a door that let out into the backyard. Many of the residents worked at the local Spitalfields market, which meant that they left for work early and often returned late. Because of this, the front doors to the buildings were usually left unlocked.

The local prostitutes knew this, of course, and exploited it to their needs. Frequently, they'd take their clients along the long passageways and into the backyards of the Hanbury Street houses. On other occasions, they would not even bother going that far and would complete the transaction in the hallways or on one of the landings.

29 Hanbury Street was typical of the houses that lined the thoroughfare. All-in-all, 17 residents were crammed into the tenement's eight rooms, while the basement housed a packing case business, run by a Mrs. Amelia Richardson. Between 4:40 a.m. and 4:45 a.m. on Saturday, 8 September, John Richardson, called at the house on his way to work. His purpose was to check on the cellar door that provided access to his mother's business. A month earlier, someone had broken the padlock. Since then, John had periodically visited the premises to ensure that all was in order.

On this particular morning, he was wearing a new pair of boots that fit uncomfortably. One of the boots was pinching his toe so he sat down on the back stairs to trim a strip of leather with a table knife. Sitting on the second step, he could clearly see that the padlock was intact. He saw nothing else unusual in the yard. Having completed the running repairs to his footwear, he went on his way.

At around 5:30 a.m., Mrs. Elizabeth Long was walking along Hanbury Street on her way to Spitalfields market when she passed a man and a woman standing outside number 29, deep in conversation. She couldn't see the man's face, but she'd later describe him as around 40 years old, of dark complexion and "foreign-looking." He was not much taller than the woman and his appearance was "shabby genteel," with a dark overcoat and a brown deerstalker hat. Mrs. Long, however, was adamant about the identity of the woman. It was Annie Chapman. As she passed, she heard the man ask, "Will you?" and the woman reply, "Yes."

A short while later, Albert Cadoche, a carpenter who lived next door at number 27, walked out into his backyard. While standing there, he heard a single word from across the fence, a woman's voice saying, "No." Cadoche then went inside but returned to the yard some three minutes later. This time, he thought that he heard something fall against the fence that divided his property from number 29. At the time, he thought nothing of it and shortly thereafter he set off for work. As he walked along nearby Commercial Street, he looked up at the clock of Christchurch Spitalfields and noticed that it was 5:32 a.m.

John Davis was an elderly carman who rented an attic room at 29 Hanbury. At around 6 a.m. on that morning, Davis came downstairs, walked along the narrow passageway and opened the door that led out into the backyard. He immediately reeled back in horror, stumbling and nearly falling before he gained his balance. Davis went running back down the passage and threw open the door leading out onto the street. He immediately encountered two workmen, James Kent and Henry Holland, and demanded of them, "Men! Come here!" Not sure what to make of this wild-eyed old man, the men followed him back into the house and down the darkened hallway.

Annie Chapman was lying on the ground between the steps and the wooden fence, her head turned towards the house. She was on her back, her skirts pulled up above her waist to expose her red and white striped stockings. Her legs were drawn up, with the feet resting on the ground and the knees turned outwards. But all of that was academic compared to the horrible mutilations that had been visited upon her. Her face was swollen with the tongue protruding between her front teeth. Her abdomen had been sliced open and the viscera pulled through the wound to above the right shoulder, although still attached. Part of the stomach had been removed and lay on the ground above the left shoulder. The throat had been deeply slashed and there was a large quantity of blood on the ground.

The three men took mere seconds to process this grim vista before racing off in different directions in search of a policeman. James Kent, though, was so shaken by what he'd seen that he soon abandoned his search and stopped off at a local pub for a large brandy to steady his nerves. Henry Holland, meanwhile, had run to the nearby Spitalfields Market and panted out his story to a constable on sentry duty. He was deeply disgusted when the bobby refused to offer assistance, saying that he was not allowed to leave his post.

It was the elderly carman, John Davis, who eventually succeeded in summoning help. He had headed directly to Commercial Street Police Station and demanded to speak to the officer in charge. Moments later Inspector Joseph Chandler was hurrying towards the scene.

*Annie Chapman*

By the time Chandler arrived, the word was out that another murder had been uncovered. A crowd of morbid onlookers had already gathered outside 29 Hanbury, with some having forced their way into the house itself. Chandler immediately called in reinforcements and had the area cleared of sightseers. He then sent for Dr. George Bagster Phillips, the Divisional Police Surgeon.

Dr. Phillips was on the scene at around 6:30 a.m. by which time the crowd outside the house had swelled to several hundred strong. A cursory glance at the body made it obvious that the victim was beyond medical help, so he set about carrying out a forensic examination.

Phillips concluded that the woman had been dead at least two hours and that she had probably been strangled, with the mutilations carried out postmortem. This time of death contradicts the witness statements of John Richardson, Elizabeth Long, and Albert Cadoche, and is almost certainly wrong. All of the evidence points to Annie Chapman having been murdered at around 5:30 a.m.

But how did Dr. Phillips, a veteran police pathologist, get this so wrong? His assessment would have been based mainly on body temperature and degree of rigor mortis. But it appears that he failed to take into account the chill of the morning and the fact that the victim had been torn open and had suffered significant blood loss. These two factors would have caused the corpse to lose heat rapidly.

That error aside, Dr. Phillip's examination produced an accurate, if horrifying, description of the corpse. That Annie Chapman was strangled there can be little doubt, scratches and a thumb imprint on her throat testified to it. Death, though, would have been due to blood loss caused by the slashes to her throat, slashes so deep they'd almost decapitated her. A spurt of arterial blood against the fence where she was found proves that she was alive (but probably unconscious) when her throat was slashed.

Further testimony as to the brutality of the crime was provided by Dr. Phillips at the inquest. The murderer had slashed Annie's throat deeply from left to right. He may have been trying to decapitate her and though he failed in this, the laceration was severe enough to cause death. The abdominal mutilations were described as follows:

*"The abdomen had been entirely laid open; the intestines, severed from their mesenteric attachments, had been lifted out of the body and placed by the shoulder of the corpse; whilst from the pelvis the*

*uterus and its appendages, with the upper portion of the vagina and the posterior two-thirds of the bladder, had been entirely removed. No trace of these parts could be found, and the incisions were cleanly cut, avoiding the rectum, and dividing the vagina low enough to avoid injury to the cervix uteri. Obviously, the work was that of an expert - of one, at least, who had such knowledge of anatomical or pathological examinations as to be enabled to secure the pelvic organs with one sweep of the knife."*

Phillips went on to say that the operation had been performed for the purpose of harvesting the body parts. He expressed surprise that the cuts could have been done so expertly, in such a short time span. He stated that he, a surgeon of 23 years' experience, would have needed fifteen minutes at least and, more likely, an hour.

Coroner Wynne E. Baxter agreed in his summation, stating that he believed the perpetrator to be someone with "considerable anatomical skill and knowledge."

There were other evidential finds at the scene. Bruises and abrasions on the dead woman's fingers suggested that some rings had been forcibly removed. A friend of Annie's would later testify that she habitually wore two brass rings. These were never found and were thus probably carried away by the killer.

Then there was an array of objects that had apparently been pulled from the victim's pockets, a square of coarse muslin, two combs, and an envelope containing a couple of pills. These had been deliberately arranged by the dead woman's feet, although the detectives were not able to determine the killer's motive for doing so. One of the more farfetched theories was that it suggested a link to freemasonry.

The Annie Chapman murder investigation was assigned to Inspector Joseph Chandler of the Metropolitan Police's H Division, with Inspector Abberline as overseer. Clearly, the top brass at the Met believed that the killer was the same man who had slaughtered Polly Nicholls.

But as in the Nicholls murder, the Chapman investigation soon became bogged down for lack of evidence. The killer had taken considerable risk, committing the crime in daylight, right across the road from the busy Spitalfields market. He had then walked calmly from the scene, most likely spattered in blood and carrying the human organs he'd just harvested. And yet no witnesses could be found who had seen anything or anyone untoward.

Of course, the investigators were not without leads, but the most important clues, provided by witnesses Richardson, Long, and Cardosch, were largely ignored because they clashed with the time of death established by the coroner. Had those leads been followed there is at least a chance that someone might have recalled seeing a man matching the description given by Elizabeth Long. They might well have noted that he'd been carrying a suspicious looking parcel, perhaps wrapped in bloody paper.

*Yard at 29 Hanbury Street where Annie Chapman was killed*

# Panic in Whitechapel

## *Aftermath of the Chapman Murder*

The murder of Annie Chapman, coming so close on the brutal killings of Polly Nicholls and Martha Tabram, cast a pall of fear and suspicion over the East End. Sensing an upswing in anti-Semitic sentiment, some local businessmen got together to form the Mile End Vigilance Committee, a sort of neighborhood watch, under the leadership of George Lusk, a local building contractor. Lusk's committee was not the only such organization to spring up in the wake of the Ripper murders, but it has become the most prominent due to the "Dear Boss" letter, purportedly from the killer, which would later be addressed to Lusk.

The Committee was comprised of 16 local tradesmen, mainly of Jewish origin. Its main objectives were to raise money for a reward and to distribute flyers asking for information. Later, its members would organize "neighborhood watch" patrols. It was soon clear, however, that the committee would fall short in its first and most important goal. Much as the citizens of Whitechapel applauded Lusk's efforts, they were not prepared to contribute to a reward fund when the government was refusing to do so.

Lusk responded by addressing an appeal directly to Queen Victoria. However, that letter was intercepted by the Home Secretary's office and Lusk received a terse reply restating the government's earlier position. The police would do everything in their power to effect a quick arrest but there would be no reward. Angered by this refusal, the Vigilance Committee secretary, Joseph Aarons, wrote an open letter to The Daily Telegraph, addressed to Home Secretary, Henry Matthews. In it, Aarons asked why the government had offered a bounty for the assassins of Lord Cavendish yet refused to "avenge the blood of these unfortunate women." Matthews didn't bother responding but Samuel Montagu, the Jewish Member of Parliament for Whitechapel, did, putting up a reward himself. It produced no tangible outcomes.

*Mr. George Lusk*

On Tuesday, September 11, a few days after the murder of Annie Chapman, John Pizer, the infamous "Leather Apron," was finally arrested. However, the police already knew that Pizer wasn't the Whitechapel murderer. Despite his proficiency with a leather knife, he didn't possess the anatomical knowledge and surgical skill that Dr. Phillips had attributed to the killer. Besides, Pizer was able to provide solid alibis for each of the murders. A rather unsavory character he may have been, but Pizer most definitely wasn't Jack the Ripper. He was soon released.

A number of other arrests followed. In the main, these were drunks who shot their mouths off about the murders while under the influence. Few of them were detained for very long.

At this time, it was difficult to go anywhere in Whitechapel and not hear some reference to the murders. People spoke in hushed tones about the monster in their midst. Wild rumors abounded. One suggested that another mutilated body had been found, this time behind the nearby London Hospital. Another was that a message had been chalked on the door at 29 Hanbury Street. "This is the fourth," it was reputed to have said. "I will murder sixteen and then give myself up."

There were reports of suspects too, generally villainous-looking men who in some way resembled the man seen by Mrs. Long. One sighting, however, bears mentioning. Mrs. Fiddymont was the wife of the owner of the Prince Albert pub, situated at the junction of Brushfield and Stewart Streets. On the early morning of the Chapman murder, a man entered the pub and asked for half a pint of ale. As Mrs. Fiddymont was drawing the pint, she observed the man in the back bar mirror. He was of middle age and medium height, with short sandy hair and a ginger moustache. Mrs. Fiddymont noticed a smear of blood under the man's right ear and a few specks of the stuff on his right hand and between his fingers. When he saw Mrs. Fiddymont watching him, he quickly gulped down the beer and left.

A pub patron, Joseph Taylor, had also noticed the man's somewhat furtive behavior. He decided to shadow the man and tracked him to Half Moon Street in Bishopsgate before losing him in the crowd. He said later that the man had appeared apprehensive and disorientated, with wild and staring eyes. As the Prince Albert is just 400 yards from the murder scene, the police were very interested in this report, although their inquiries ultimately came up empty. The man with the ginger moustache would, however, be mentioned again, in connection with another Ripper murder.

Reports such as these, not to mention lurid (and often reckless) reporting by the newspapers, served to infuse the entire East End with a palpable sense of panic. For a time, darkness brought about an unofficial curfew, with the streets all but deserted, save for the patrolling bobbies. Yet, even with a homicidal maniac on the loose, it didn't take long for Whitechapel's bawdy nightlife to return to its usual raucous level. Too many people's livelihoods depended on it.

Then, just when things began to approach normality again, came another horrific development, one that would have a profound effect on the case and on Ripper folklore.

On September 27, 1888, a letter arrived at the offices of the Central News Agency. Written in red ink, it read as follows:

*25 Sept 1888*

*Dear Boss*

*I keep on hearing the police have caught me but they wont fix me just yet. I have laughed when they look so clever and talk about being on the right track. That joke about Leather Apron gave me real fits. I am down on whores and I shant quit ripping them till I do get buckled. Grand work the last job was. I gave the lady no time to squeal. How can they catch me now. I love my work and want to start again. You will soon hear of me with my funny little games. I saved some proper red stuff in a ginger beer bottle over the last job to write with but it went thick like glue and I cant use it. Red ink is fit enough I hope ha.ha. The next job I do I shall clip. The lady's ears off and send to the Police officers just for jolly wouldn't you. Keep this letter back till I do a bit more work then give it out straight. My knife's so nice and sharp I want to get to work right away if I get a chance.*

*Good luck.*

*Yours truly*

*Jack the Ripper*

*Don't mind me giving the trade name*

This letter, along with another sent to George Lusk of the Mile End Vigilance Committee nearly three weeks later, has become as much part of Ripper folklore as the murders themselves. These days you won't find a Ripper expert who considers them to be genuine. Even back then, their origins were considered dubious. However, they did achieve one thing, they gave the Whitechapel murderer his terrifying nom de guerre.

# Strike Three

## *The Murder of Long Liz Stride*

The "Dear Boss" letter may have been a hoax but the warning contained therein: *"I love my work and want to start again,"* turned out to be a portent of real evil to come. Just three days after the letter was delivered, the Ripper struck again, this time claiming two victims in a single night.

Elizabeth Stride, known to her friends as "Long Liz," was a Swedish immigrant who worked as a domestic servant and sometimes supplemented her paltry earnings through prostitution. On the last day of her life, Elizabeth spent the afternoon cleaning rooms at a lodging house, earning sixpence for her labor. By 6:30 p.m., she was drinking away those earnings in the Queen's Head pub at the corner of Fashion and Commercial Streets. Later she returned to her lodgings, leaving the premises at around 7:30 dressed "for a night out," in the words of one of her fellow residents.

The next sighting of Elizabeth was at around eleven o'clock when she was seen taking shelter from a downpour in the doorway of the Bricklayer's Arms pub on Settles Street. She wasn't alone. There was a man with her, around 5 foot 5 inches tall with a black moustache, dressed respectably in a black morning suit. She and the man were entwined in a passionate embrace. Two passersby, Best and Gardner, couldn't resist ribbing the couple. "Watch out, that's Leather Apron getting round you," Best called out jovially.

The couple then rushed off into the rain, in the direction of Commercial Road.

Elizabeth Stride must have parted with her beau soon after, because at around 11:45 p.m., a laborer named William Marshall spotted her outside number 63 Berner Street, with a different man. This one was middle-aged, stoutly built and clean shaven. Marshall heard the man say to the woman, "You would say anything but your prayers," before the couple walked off in the direction of Dutfield's Yard.

At 12:30 a.m., PC William Smith was walking his beat along Berner Street when he spotted Stride standing with a man outside Dutfield's Yard, where her body would later be found. This man was described as late-twenties, with a dark complexion and a small dark moustache. He was about five foot seven and wearing dark clothing and a deerstalker hat. As the couple was doing nothing to arouse PC Smith's suspicions, he passed by without saying anything to them. Liz Stride had only minutes to live.

At around 12:45, a man named Israel Schwartz was walking along Berner Street in the direction of the International Working Men's Educational Club, a social club for Jewish workers. Walking some distance ahead of him was a man, about 5 feet, 5 inches tall, aged around 30 with dark hair, a fair complexion, a small brown moustache. He had a full face, broad shoulders and appeared to be slightly intoxicated. As Schwartz watched, the man approached a woman, standing in the doorway of Dutfield's Yard. A few words were exchanged before the man tried to pull the woman into the street. Then he spun her around and pushed her to the ground.

Schwartz was convinced that he was witnessing a domestic dispute. Not wanting to get involved, he crossed the road. It was then that he spotted a second man, standing in the shadows, lighting his pipe. As Schwartz passed him, the man who was attacking the woman called out to this second man, "Lipski!" The second man then started following Schwartz, causing him to panic and run.

Israel Schwartz would later relate this story both to the police and to the press. However, he spoke no English and had to converse via a translator, resulting perhaps in some of the details being lost in translation. As a result, his story varied with each retelling and the police all but dismissed it.

But what are we to make of the story over a century later? There seems to be no reason for Schwartz to have made up such a fanciful tale, making it likely that the man he saw attacking Elizabeth Stride was, in fact, Jack the Ripper. But what then of the second man? Are we to believe that the Ripper had an accomplice? The evidence suggests not. In fact, in a report published on October 19, 1888, Chief Inspector Swanson stated that the police had traced the "second man" and cleared him of any involvement in the murder.

So the man seen by Schwartz attacking Elizabeth Stride was acting alone and it is quite possible that Schwartz, in his panicked state, misread the situation. Fifteen minutes after Schwartz witnessed the altercation, "Long Liz" would be immortalized as Jack the Ripper's third victim.

At 1 a.m. Louis Diemshutz, steward of the International Working Men's Educational Club, returned to Dutfield's Yard from Westow Hill Market where he operated a stall selling cheap jewelry. As he entered the yard, his pony suddenly reared up and refused to go any further. Looking into the darkness, Diemshutz spotted the source of the horse's distress, a crumpled shape lying on the ground close to the wall of the club. Prodding at it with his whip produced no result so he dismounted and went to investigate.

It was windy that evening, and when Diemshutz struck a match, it was quickly extinguished by a gust. However, the brief flicker of flame was enough for him to make out the form of a woman. He then dashed into the club to summon help. "There's a woman lying in the yard," he told startled club members, "but I cannot say whether she is drunk or dead." That questioned would be answered seconds later when Diemshutz re-entered the yard in the company of several club members. The candle he held made a poor beacon. It provided enough light, however, to see the horrific injuries inflicted on the woman's throat.

Diemshutz and the other club members immediately dispersed to find a constable and their cries of "Murder!" and "Police!" quickly attracted the attention of PC Edward Spooner. By the time the group returned to the yard with Spooner in tow, a crowd of around fifteen had already gathered. Spooner stooped to examine the victim, noting that her skin was still warm. Then he lifted her chin and saw the deep slashes to her throat which was later described by him as, "fearfully cut."

*Elizabeth Stride*

The next two police officers to arrive at Dutfield's Yard were Constables Henry Lamb and Edward Collins. The crowd had now swelled to about 30 people and Lamb ordered them back, warning that if they got blood on their clothes, they might find themselves with some difficult questions to answer. He then told Collins to fetch Dr. Frederick William Blackwell who lived nearby at 100 Commercial Street. Morris Eagle, one of the club members, was sent to Leman Street Police Station to summon further assistance.

Dr. Blackwell arrived in the Yard at 1:16 a.m. and after a quick examination pronounced the woman dead, adding that she had probably died 20 to 30 minutes earlier. Cause of death was a long cut to the neck, starting on the left, severing the blood vessels there, cutting right through the windpipe and terminating on the opposite side. At the subsequent inquest, Dr. Blackwell would offer the opinion that the killer had grabbed the woman by the scarf she was wearing around her neck and had pulled her backward before slicing through her windpipe and vocal chords, rendering her unable to cry out. Given the severity of the wound, she would have bled to death within 90 seconds.

While Dr. Blackwell was examining the corpse, the police officers had got to work processing the scene. In those days, such measures were cursory at best, but PC Lamb had the presence of mind to order that the gates into Dutfield's Yard be shut with all onlookers inside. He and PC Collins them made their way through the crowd, examining hands and clothing for traces of blood. They next carried out a search of the club before walking to the cottages that backed onto the club and rousing the residents from sleep. No one had seen or heard anything.

By the time Lamb and Collins returned, Inspectors West and Pinhorn had arrived, along with police pathologist Dr. Phillips. A quick conference between the two doctors and the senior police officers narrowed the time of death to a sixteen-minute interval between 12:36 and 12:56 a.m. It appeared that Louis Diemshutz had interrupted the Ripper at his work, leaving his bloodlust unsated. That, regrettably, would have dreadful consequences for another woman.

*Entrance to Dutfield's Yard*

# Kate Eddowes Comes to Grief

## *The Mitre Square Atrocity*

Mitre Square is a small, cobble-stoned quadrant of some 24 yards by 24, surrounded mainly by commercial buildings and warehouses, with only a few residences. Lying within the bounds of the City of London, the Square is some three-quarters of a mile, or a twenty-minute walk, from Dutfield's Yard. At night, when the businesses were closed, it was a dark and secluded place. In the early morning hours of September 30, 1888, it would become the scene of a horrific murder.

*Mitre Square*

Like the three earlier Ripper victims, Catherine Eddowes was a prostitute. She was also an alcoholic who drank away most of her earnings and was prone to eccentric behavior when inebriated. It was this that had gotten her into trouble on the evening of September 29, when she had been arrested on Aldgate High Street while entertaining a crowd of onlookers with a drunken imitation of a fire engine. Hauled off to Bishopsgate Police Station she was pushed into a cell and told to "sleep it off."

Catherine, or Kate as she was known, spent the next few hours fast asleep. But by 12:15, she was awake and belting out a bawdy ditty. PC George Hutt, the officer on duty, went to the cell and told her to pipe down, at which Kate demanded to know when she was to be released. "When you can take care of yourself," Hutt responded, to which Eddowes called back, "I can do that now."

PC Hutt must have been unconvinced by this assertion because he held Kate for another 40 minutes before eventually giving in to her loud pleas for release at 12:55 a.m. As she was being ushered from the station, she asked Hutt what time it was. "Too late for you to get any more drink," Hutt observed.

"I shall get a damned fine hiding when I get home," Kate sighed, to which Hutt replied that she probably deserved it. "You have no right to get drunk," he said. "Good night old cock," was Kate's only response as she stepped out into the damp morning and started towards Houndsditch, following a path that would bring her to Mitre Square within eight minutes. At that very moment, the killer of Elizabeth Stride was also approaching the square, coming from the opposite direction.

One of the officers walking the Aldgate beat that night was PC Edward Watkins. Watkins' route took him through Mitre Square every twelve to fourteen minutes and when he passed through at 1:30 a.m. he shone his lantern around the small quadrant and saw nothing out of the ordinary.

Some minutes later, Harry Harris, Joseph Hyam Levy and Joseph Lawende were walking along Duke Street after leaving the Imperial Club. At the corner of Church Street, they spotted a man and a woman talking intimately together, the woman with her hand resting on the man's chest. Harris and Levy paid the couple scant attention and were later unable to describe either of the individuals.

Joseph Lawende, however, was more observant. He would later swear that the woman he saw was Catherine Eddowes.

As for the man, Lawende was able to provide a detailed description, despite the poor street lighting. He said that the man was about 30 years old and had the "appearance of a sailor." He was about 5-foot-9 in height and of medium build, fair complexioned with a small, moustache. He had on a loose fitting jacket and wore a gray cloth cap. A reddish neckerchief was knotted around his throat. This description was incredibly thorough, given that Lawende had only a brief glimpse of the man in poor light. He was almost certainly mistaken in some aspects, but given that Catherine Eddowes' body was discovered just fifteen minutes later in Mitre Square, it seems highly likely that Joseph Lawende was one of the few to see the face of Jack the Ripper.

At 1:44 a.m., mere minutes after Joseph Lawende had seen the couple talking together, PC Edward Watkins was back on his circular route and entering Mitre Square from the southeast. When he'd passed through fifteen minutes earlier, he'd seen nothing untoward. Now, as he shone his lantern into a dark corner, he made a horrific discovery.

The body of a woman lay on the ground, positioned on her back with her feet facing in towards the square. Her clothes were pulled up above her waist. Her throat was cut and her stomach ripped open, her intestines protruding from the gaping wound. Her face, too, had suffered severe lacerations and there was blood pooled around her.

Watkins reeled back in horror, then turned and raced across the square towards Kearley and Tonge's warehouse, where he knew the night watchman, a retired police officer named George Morris. "For God's sake mate!" Watkins cried, "Come to my assistance. Here is another woman cut to pieces."

Snatching up his lamp, the night watchman followed Watkins to the southwest corner of the square, took one look at the body, and sprinted off along Mitre Street in the direction of Aldgate, blowing furiously on his whistle. The ruckus soon alerted the attention of PCs Harvey and Holland who returned with him to Mitre Square to view the carnage. Then Holland ran to fetch Dr. George Sequeira from his home on nearby Jewry Street.

Sequeira was at the scene by 1:55 and didn't even bother checking for a pulse, declaring only that death had been instantaneous and that he did not believe that the killer had any anatomical skill. He then waited on the arrival of City Police Divisional Surgeon, Dr. Frederick Gordon Brown who would later conduct a detailed postmortem, detailing the full horrific nature of the murder. Significantly, Brown would differ from Sequeira in his opinion of the killer's level of anatomical expertise. He believed that the perpetrator had "considerable knowledge of the position of the organs in the abdominal cavity and the way of removing them."

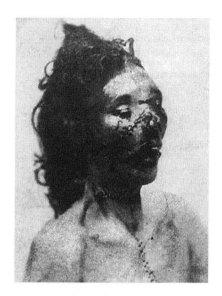

*Catherine Eddowes*

Meanwhile, Inspector Edward Collard had arrived from Bishopsgate Police Station and ordered an immediate search, with door-to-door inquiries to be made of the area surrounding Mitre Square. Next, Superintendent James McWilliam, Head of Detectives for the City Police Department, arrived with a detachment of his men, who he immediately dispersed to carry out a search of the Spitalfields streets and lodging houses. They encountered several men on their path, all of whom were stopped and questioned to no avail. The killer, it seemed, had simply disappeared.

Ironically, the only residence on Mitre Square at the time of the murder was occupied by a City of London Police Constable named Richard Pearse. But Pearse had neither seen nor heard anything. Neither had George Morris, the night watchman whose whistle had sounded the alarm.

As an article in the Illustrated Police News reported it:

*"He (Morris) could hear the footsteps of the policeman as he passed on his beat every quarter of an hour, so that it appeared impossible that the woman could have uttered any sound without his detecting it. It was only on the night that he remarked to some policeman that he wished the "butcher" would come round Mitre Square and he would give him a doing; yet the butcher had come and he was perfectly ignorant of it."*

Perhaps even stranger was the fact that at the very moment that Catherine Eddowes was entering Mitre Square with her murderer, three City detectives – Daniel Halse, Robert Outram, and Edward Marriot – were patrolling along Mitre Street in the vicinity of the square and saw nothing.

The body of Catherine Eddowes was removed for autopsy to Golden Lane Mortuary, where Dr. Brown carried out the examination. As with Polly Nichols and Annie Chapman, Eddowes' throat had been deeply slashed from left to right. The resulting wound was the cause of death, but there were severe postmortem mutilations, best described by Dr. Brown's testimony.

*"The abdomen had been laid open from the breast bone to the pubes. The intestines had been detached to a large extent and about two feet of the colon was cut away. The peritoneal lining was cut through and the left kidney carefully taken out and removed. The left renal artery was cut through. I should say that someone who knew the position of the kidney must have done it. The womb was*

*cut through horizontally, leaving a stump of ¾ of an inch. The rest of the womb had been taken away with some of the ligaments. The vagina and cervix of the womb was uninjured.*

*"The face was very much mutilated. There was a cut about ¼ of an inch through the lower left eyelid dividing the structures. The right eyelid was cut through to about ½ inch. There was a deep cut over the bridge of the nose extending from the left border of the nasal bone down near to the angle of the jaw of the right side. The tip of the nose was quite detached from the nose.*

*"Several other cuts were sustained on the face, plus the right ear lobe had been completely severed and had fallen from her clothing when she was taken to the morgue."*

The nature of these injuries led Dr. Brown to conclude that the killer had known exactly which organs he wanted and had excised them expertly.

# The Writing on the Wall

*A Strip of Apron and the Goulston Street Graffito*

After murdering Catherine Eddowes, the Whitechapel Murderer fled east from Mitre Square, along Aldgate. This seems a strange decision, given the concentration of police in this area, but the Ripper was quite obviously confident of outmaneuvering his pursuers in an area that he knew well. How do we know that he went east? Because of a piece of evidence that was found in a doorway in Goulston Street, just a short distance from Mitre Square.

The clue was a strip of bloody apron, discovered by PC Alfred Long while walking his beat along Goulston Street at 2:55 a.m. on the morning of the murder. The fabric was later determined to have been cut from the apron that Catherine Eddowes was wearing when she died. Most likely, the killer had taken it to wipe blood from his hands or from his blade. PC Long had, in fact, walked passed the same spot at 2:20, and had noticed nothing untoward. So had Detective Daniel Halse, and he too had seen nothing out of the ordinary. That suggests that the killer must have dropped it sometime between 2:20 and 2:55, half and hour to an hour after Catherine Eddowes was killed. That tells us quite a lot about the Ripper. First that he knew the area extremely well, and second that he was confident in his ability to stay one step ahead of the police, perhaps even disdainful of their attempts to catch him. Why else would he stay out on the streets with half of the City of London police force hunting him? This type of risk-seeking behavior is quite common in psychopaths.

The strip of apron tells us something else about the murders. Originally it was assumed that the Ripper would have been covered in blood after carrying out his gory mutilations. But a simple evaluation of the evidence suggests otherwise. The small strip of cloth that he cut from the apron tells us that he didn't have much blood to clean up. How can that be? It's quite simple really.

These days, it is generally accepted that the Ripper strangled his victims into submission. By the time he started cutting, the victim was either dead or the heart had slowed to such an extent that there was either no spurt of arterial blood or the spurt of blood was weak. This was observed at all of the crime scenes. As for the blood he'd have got on him while mutilating his victims, it is likely that he'd have been wearing an overcoat, which he removed before carrying out the murder, ostensibly to enable him to engage in sex with the victim. Then when he was done, he'd put the coat back on, thus hiding any bloodstains to his clothing. It must be remembered that he walked away from the Annie Chapman crime scene in broad daylight and followed a path that ran directly past the bustling Spitalfields market, and yet attracted not one suspicious glance.

The strip of apron thus answers a number of questions about the Ripper's modus operandi and possibly tells us something about his personality. But there was another clue discovered that night, one that throws up as many questions as the apron answers.

I am referring, of course, to the infamous graffito found scrawled on a Goulston Street wall, directly above where the piece of apron was found. Written in chalk, it read:

*"The Juwes are the men that will not be blamed for nothing."*

Much has been made of that single line of semi-literate scrawl. Was it written by the Ripper, and if so, to what purpose? There have been three possible explanations offered.

The first was that the message was not written by the murderer at all and that when he tossed the piece of apron away and it fell fortuitously beside the meaningless graffito. The message thus had nothing to do with the case.

The second was that the message was written by the killer and that it was a kind of triumphalism. Flushed with his "success" at carrying out the double murder, he was boasting to the police and at the same time defiantly identifying himself as a Jew. It was even suggested at the time that "Juwes" was the Yiddish spelling of Jews, although this was dispelled by the local chief Rabbi and easily disproven.

The final interpretation, the one favored by Scotland Yard, was that the message was written by the killer to deflect attention away from himself. He was not a Jew but he was aware that most locals believed the murders to be the work of a "foreigner." Thus he scrawled the message to fan the flames of anti-Semitism. The fact that the building the message was scrawled on housed mostly single Jewish men, was cited as credence for this theory. It was the acceptance of this idea that fueled the controversial next move in the investigation.

With the City and Metropolitan police forces clashing over what should be done with the graffito (the City wanted it photographed; the Met insisted that it should be obliterated immediately), the matter was referred to Police Commissioner Sir Charles Warren. Warren arrived to inspect the site at 5:30 a.m. and immediately sided with the Metropolitan Police. The message was to be erased without delay, with no photograph taken to preserve it.

Thus, a potentially vital clue to the identity of Jack the Ripper was lost. Warren later defended his actions in a report to the Home office on November 6, 1888. He feared, he said, an outpouring of violent retribution against the Jewish population, if the message were to be seen by Gentiles. As it would be light within minutes and the streets would soon be filling with people, he had felt that there was no time to lose in getting rid of the message.

Was Warren right to do so? In retrospect, he probably was. Most who saw the message commented that it was slightly faded and therefore not of recent vintage. It also seems unlikely that the Ripper would have stood out in the open scrawling a message on the wall while the police were swarming through the area searching for him. In any case, the controversy over the erased message would soon be eclipsed as another Ripper letter arrived, this one marked, "From Hell."

# Dear Boss

## *Letters from Hell*

Although two letters, in particular, have received prominence in the Jack the Ripper case, the police, newspapers, and authorities received upwards of 700 over the course of the investigation. Many of these were from concerned citizens offering advice and suggestions on how to catch the killer, but a not insignificant number (as many as 300) purported to come from Jack himself.

Of these letters, most were quite obviously hoaxes, and rightfully derided as such. But that is not to say that all were insignificant to the case. For example, the "Dear Boss" letter, which arrived at the offices of the Central News Agency on September 27, had the noteworthy outcome of giving the killer his infamous nickname. Up until the murders of Elizabeth Stride and Catherine Eddowes on September 30, 1888, the unidentified killer had been known variously as the "Whitechapel Murderer," the "Red Fiend" or "Leather Apron." But the Dear Boss letter offered a much catchier suggestion. It was signed "Jack the Ripper," and it is under that terrifying nom de guerre that the killer would attain lasting infamy.

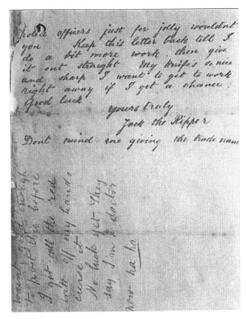

*Dear Boss Letter*

The "Dear Boss" letter had initially been given the same treatment as the many crank missives regarding the case. But after the double murder, the police had cause to study it more closely.

*"I want to get to work right away if I get a chance,"* the letter had stated, and it appeared that the killer had done just that. More significantly, he'd threatened, *"The next job I do I shall clip. The lady's ears off and send to the Police officers just for jolly wouldn't you."* One of Catherine Eddowes' earlobes had indeed been cut off, and that appeared too much of a coincidence. So had the letter been written by the killer after all?

Senior police officers were divided on the issue. But with the investigation floundering, with harsh criticism in the press, with the public up in arms over the latest murders, with nary a clue to hunt down, they decided to release the letter to the newspapers. Perhaps someone would recognize the handwriting or pick up on the unique diction.

So it was that, on October 1, the "Dear Boss" letter appeared in its entirety in all of the main London dailies. It precipitated a deluge of new tips and a number of new hoax letters, including a postcard that arrived at the Central News Agency on Monday, October 1.

Written in red ink and in a hand that was similar to that of the "Dear Boss" letter, the card was also specked with what appeared to be bloodstains. It bore a postmark dated October 1 and read as follows:

*"I was not codding dear old Boss when I gave you the tip, you'll hear about Saucy Jacky's work tomorrow double event this time number one squealed a bit couldn't finish straight off had not the time to get ears for police. thanks for keeping last letter back till I got to work again.*

*Jack the Ripper"*

The inference of these words was that the killer had penned them shortly after killing Liz Stride and Kate Eddowes and before the murders were public knowledge. That seemed to prove its authenticity and the decision was again taken to publish it. But that tactic would backfire badly as the police were quickly swamped by a deluge of hoax letters and worthless tips. All of these, of course, had to be checked out, pulling massive manpower away from potentially more fruitful avenues of investigation.

As October continued with no further progress in the case, more and more letters continued to arrive in the mailboxes of police officers and newsmen. Then, on October 16, a letter arrived at the residence of Mr. George Lusk, President of the Mile End Vigilance Committee. Addressed, "From Hell" it is arguably the most infamous of the Ripper letters.

Lusk, of course, is a prominent figure in Ripper folklore. His committee had begun running patrols in the area after the "double event," while Lusk himself had addressed several public gatherings and was still actively soliciting the Home Secretary urging a rethink of the "no reward" policy. Lusk had also been featured several times in the newspapers, talking about the case.

All of this publicity drew unwanted attention. By mid-October Lusk had reported to police that he was being stalked by a "mysterious stranger." He also received two letters, each purporting to be from Jack the Ripper. Then, on Tuesday, October 16, Lusk received a small package, wrapped in brown paper and bearing a London postmark. The package gave off an odd smell and it was soon clear why. Inside was half a human kidney. There was also a letter, which read:

*"From hell*

*Mr Lusk*

*Sor*

*I send you half the Kidne I took from one women prasarved it for you tother piece I fried and ate it was very nise I may send you the bloody knif that took it out if you only wate a whil longer*

*signed Catch me when you Can*

*Mishter Lusk"*

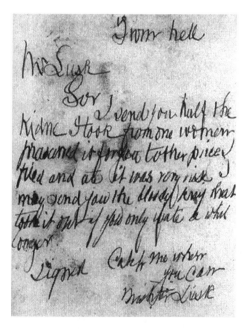

*From Hell letter*

Lusk's initial reaction was that the letter was another sick prank and that the kidney was likely from an animal. Nonetheless, he decided to seek a medical opinion and thus carried the package to the Mile End Road surgery, where a Dr. Reed examined the kidney and stated that, in his opinion, it was human. He suggested, however, that Lusk obtain a second opinion and the kidney was therefore taken to the London Hospital where Dr. Thomas Openshaw, the Pathological Curator, examined it.

Openshaw confirmed that the specimen was indeed human but stressed that there was no way of proving who it was from or even whether it was from a man or a woman. His opinion was that it had more than likely come from a cadaver procured for medical dissection and was the subject of a prank perpetrated by some medical student.

To the press, however, the confirmation that the kidney was human was all that mattered. This latest macabre twist, together with the suggestion of cannibalism contained in the "From Hell" letter, was too good a story to pass up. Over the days that followed, the papers printed vastly inaccurate versions of Dr. Openshaw's diagnosis. The kidney was reported as being from a woman of about 45 years of age, "not yet three weeks dead," and a heavy drinker with a preference for gin. This, undoubtedly, was meant to suggest that the organ was from Kate Eddowes, although that was never an opinion offered by Dr. Openshaw.

The next medical man to examine the kidney was Dr. Gordon Brown, a pathologist attached to the City Police Force. He too offered the opinion that it was human but did not elaborate on its origin, which in that era would have been impossible to determine. He did, however, say that he agreed with Openshaw's assessment that the whole affair was likely a hoax perpetrated by a medical student.

One final misconception about the kidney needs to be cleared up. It has been stated in a number of books on the case that the organ showed signs of advanced Bright's disease, an affliction that Kate Eddowes supposedly suffered from. This has been reported so frequently that it is now widely regarded as fact. Yet the origins of this story are tenuous, to say the least. As far as can be established, it originates in the memoirs of Major Henry Smith, acting City Commissioner. Smith attributes this diagnosis to Mr. Sutton, a senior surgeon at London Hospital and a renowned authority on diseases of the kidneys.

However, no written report by Sutton has survived to back up Smith's claim, if he ever made it in the first place. Major Smith it appears was prone to exaggeration, with a reputation for being somewhat economical with the truth when it stood in the way of a good story. Most of the doctors who examined the kidney in the day held fast to the opinion that it was not from Catherine Eddowes. There appears no valid reason to second guess them.

But what of the Ripper letters? Was any of them penned by the elusive Jack? There is no evidence to suggest that they were. The "Dear Boss" letter, in fact, has been attributed to Thomas J. Bulling, a journalist who worked at the Central News Agency. As for the "Letter from Hell," who knows? Hoax letter writing was to become almost a national obsession during the Ripper investigation and there is little reason to believe that this one letter was any more authentic than the hundreds of others that poured in.

# Massacre in Miller's Court

## *The Horrific Murder of Mary Kelly*

In the weeks following the "Double Event," Whitechapel again went into a state of virtual lockdown. The once rowdy streets were all but deserted after dark with many of the prostitutes leaving the area and finding lodgings with friends or family elsewhere. Legitimate trade also suffered. Many Londoners were afraid even to set foot in Whitechapel, for fear of falling into the hands of a monster whose legend had by now assumed near mythic proportions.

The police response was emphatic. Uniformed and plainclothes officers flooded into the area, walking the streets during the hours of darkness. In this endeavor, they were ably assisted by Mr. Lusk's Mile End Vigilance Committee, who hired local men to patrol the darkened yards and alleys, equipped with billy clubs and police whistles.

By day, police officers systematically worked their way through the area's many lodging houses. Over 2,000 lodgers were questioned, with special attention being paid to individuals working in certain occupations. Some 76 butchers and slaughterers were interrogated, plus many sailors working on the Thames River boats. A team of bloodhounds was also deployed, in the hope that they might somehow sniff out the killer.

Another measure employed by the authorities was to distribute 80,000 handbills throughout the neighborhood:

*"POLICE NOTICE*

*TO THE OCCUPIER*

*On the morning of Friday, 31st August, Saturday 8th, and Sunday, 30th September, 1888, Women were murdered in or near Whitechapel, supposed by some one residing in the immediate neighborhood. Should you know of any person to whom suspicion is attached, you are earnestly requested to communicate at once with the nearest Police Station, Metropolitan Police Office, 30th September, 1888."*

This triggered a new flood of leads, many coming from vengeful wives and jilted lovers who reported their partners out of spite. But it produced no real clues.

Neither did any of the other methods help in capturing the elusive Jack. They did, however, have the effect of calming tensions in Whitechapel. A month passed without another murder. The streets gradually got back to normal and the prostitutes returned to ply their trade. But if the people of Whitechapel believed that the Ripper had moved on, they were about to be proved wrong – in the most brutal of fashions.

Mary Kelly was a 25-year-old Irish prostitute, who had arrived in London from her hometown of Limerick. People who knew Mary, said that she was tall and pretty, a view later echoed by the Daily

Telegraph who described her as "fair of complexion, with light hair, and possessing rather attractive features."  She appears also to have been well-liked and respected in the area. Most spoke of her pleasant demeanor, although some noted that she could be abusive when under the influence.


Mary rented a first floor room at Miller's Court in Dorset Street, Spitalfields, but at the beginning of November 1888, she was beset by money problems and several weeks behind with the rent. Her lover, Joe Barnett, was of no help either, unemployed and flat broke. Kelly and Barnett had recently had an argument and he'd moved out of their shared room. But the spat was short-lived. On Thursday night, November 8, Barnett visited Mary at Miller's Court and apologized for his behavior and for not having any money to give her. His apology was apparently accepted and he spent about an hour with Mary, leaving at around 7:45 to return to his lodgings in Bishopsgate. There he played a few hands of whisk with other residents before retiring at around 12:30.

*Mary Kelly's room in Miller's Court*

At around 10:45 the following morning, Mary Kelly's landlord, John McCarthy, sent his assistant Thomas Bowyer to 13 Miller's Court to collect Mary's overdue rent. Bowyer duly arrived at Miller's Court where he banged twice on the door but got no answer. Believing that Mary was hiding inside, he walked to the bedroom window, where there was a broken pane. Reaching through, he grabbed the edge of a curtain and pulled it aside. Moments later, he staggered back, ashen-faced. Then he turned and ran.

Landlord John McCarthy was at his nearby shop when Bowyer staggered through the door. "Guv'nor," he stammered. "I think you'd better come take a look." Pressed for details, Bowyer would only say that there was a "lot of blood." The two men then hurried together towards Miller's Court.

McCarthy had been convinced that his assistant was either mistaken or exaggerating. But a look into the gloomy interior quickly disavowed him of that view. Mary Kelly's bedroom looked like the interior of an abattoir. The wall behind the bed was liberally spattered with blood, while on the bedside table was a gory pile that appeared to be human flesh. But that wasn't even the worst of it. A figure lay on the bed, a figure so drenched in blood, so severely mutilated that it was barely recognizable as human.

McCarthy reeled back, sucking in breaths of air and struggling to keep from ejecting his breakfast onto the ground. "I cannot drive that sight from my mind," he later told a journalist, "It looked more like the work of a devil than of a man."

It took a moment for John McCarthy to regain some composure. Once he did, he dispatched Bowyer to the nearby Commercial Street Police Station to fetch a police officer. Inspectors Dew and Beck were chatting inside the station when Bowyer staggered through the door. "It's the Ripper," Bowyer managed to get out. "He's done another one."

Beck and Dew were soon following Bowyer back towards Dorset Street. When they arrived at Miller's Court, they tried the door and found it locked. Inspector Beck then went to the window and peered into the room. Almost immediately he reeled away. "For God's sake Dew, don't look," he told his colleague.

Dew, however, did look, taking in a vista that would remain with him for the rest of his days. Describing it in his memoirs fifty years later, he wrote:

*"As my thoughts go back to Miller's Court, and what happened there, the old nausea, indignation and horror overwhelm me still. My mental picture of it remains as shockingly clear as though it were but yesterday. No savage could have been more barbaric. No wild animal could have done anything so horrifying."*

Inspector Abberline, summoned by Dew, was the next police officer on the scene, arriving in the company of police surgeon, Dr. George Bagster Phillips. After obtaining a key from John McCarthy, the officers entered the small, cluttered room, where Mary's body lay on the bed, so severely mutilated that even a veteran police officer like Abberline, and an experienced surgeon like Phillips, found it difficult to look at the corpse. Indeed, Mary was so horrifically disfigured that when her lover Joe Barnett was later brought in to identify the body, he could only do so by recognizing Mary's eyes.

The extent of these mutilations is best described by the medical examiner's report, filed by veteran pathologist Dr. Thomas Bond.

*"The body was lying naked in the middle of the bed, the shoulders flat, but the axis of the body inclined to the left side of the bed. The whole of the surface of the abdomen and thighs was removed and the abdominal cavity emptied of its viscera. The breasts were cut off, the arms mutilated by several jagged wounds and the face hacked beyond recognition of the features and the tissues of the neck were*

*severed all round down to the bone. The viscera were found in various parts: the uterus and kidney with one breast under the head, the other breast by the right foot, the liver between the feet, the intestines by the right side and the spleen by the left side. The flaps removed from the abdomen and thighs were on a table.*

*"Her face was gashed in all directions, the nose, cheeks, eyebrows & ears being partly removed. The lips were blanched and cut by several incisions running obliquely down to the chin. There were also numerous cuts extending irregularly across all of the features.*

*"The skin and tissues of the abdomen from the costal arch to the pubes were removed in three large flaps. The right thigh was denuded in front to the bone, the flap of skin including the external organs of generation and part of the right buttock. The left thigh was stripped of skin, fascia & muscles as far as the knee."*

*Mary Kelly's horribly mutilated corpse*

Dr. Bond's report continued for several more paragraphs cataloging in minute detail the ferocious destruction of Mary Kelly's body. Not all of the organs were accounted for and it was assumed that the killer had carried these (including the heart) away with him.

Cause of death was given as severance of the carotid artery with all of the mutilations carried out postmortem. As to the time of death, Dr. Bond judged this to have occurred between one and two o'clock in the morning. He stressed, however, that this was approximate given the time that had elapsed between the murder and the discovery of the body.

There seemed little doubt that the man who had killed Mary Kelly was the same monster who was responsible for the other four recently committed murders. All of the women had been killed with a very sharp knife of at least six inches in length and an inch in width. Dr. Bond's next assertion, however, appeared to throw some doubt on that idea.

In three of the earlier murders, the pathologist had concluded that the killer must have had some degree of medical training in order to carry out the mutilations that he did. Bond, however, was emphatic when asked that question. He said that killer possessed no anatomical knowledge at all, not even that of a butcher or horse slaughterer.

This, of course, is starkly different to the conclusions drawn by other medical experts. So what might have influenced Bond's opinion? Many Ripper experts believe that Dr. Bond found it difficult to accept that a member of his profession could have committed such atrocious acts. Most take the view that Jack knew where and how to cut to remove his trophies. And that points to someone who had at least some medical training.

As news of the Miller murder began filtering out, a new wave of panic swept through Whitechapel and the streets were once again abandoned to the police patrols. That sense of anxiety soon spilled over into violence and there were sporadic incidents of vigilantism, directed at anyone thought to be acting suspiciously. Inevitably, pressure was piled on the police to bring the reign of terror to an end. Even Queen Victoria weighed in to criticize their lack of progress.

Yet the absence of tangible results was by no means due to want of trying. The investigation had by now become the largest murder inquiry in British history. The police followed up every lead, chased down and interrogated every suspect, kept up its street patrols and even put officers under cover, disguised as prostitutes. All of it came to nothing. The murderer had left behind not a clue, and while there were a number of eyewitnesses, a disagreement between the physicians as to time of death, complicated things. Dr. Bond believed that Mary Kelly had been killed between 1 a.m. and 2 a.m., Dr. Phillips felt it was later, between 4 and 5.

One of the witnesses, George Hutchinson, seemed to verify the later time. Hutchinson was a laborer who knew Mary Kelly. According to him, he'd encountered Mary at around 2 a.m. on Friday morning. She'd asked him for some money and when he said he had none she'd walked away, stopping within a short distance to talk to another man.

According to Hutchinson, the man placed his arm around Mary's shoulders and they set off together, walking towards Dorset Street. He followed at a distance and saw them stop and talk for about three minutes. The man said something to Mary and she replied, "Alright my dear, come along, you will be comfortable." The man then placed his arm on Mary's shoulder and kissed her. They walked from there to Mary's room and entered. Hutchinson waited outside for about 40 minutes to see if they would come out again. When they didn't, he left.

Asked to describe the man, Hutchinson said that he was mid-thirties, about 5-foot-6, with dark eyes, dark hair, and a small moustache. He was wearing a long dark coat, light waistcoat, dark trousers, and a dark felt hat turned down in the middle. He was very respectable looking with a "Jewish appearance."

Several other people reported seeing Mary on the night she died. Mary Ann Cox, another prostitute, saw Mary going into Miller's Court with a man at 11:45 p.m. Mary was very drunk, according to Cox. The man was described as about 36 years old, about 5-foot-6, with a pale complexion and blotches on his face. He had small side-whiskers, and a thick "carroty" moustache. He was dressed in shabby, dark clothes, dark overcoat, and black felt hat.

Laundress Sarah Lewis said that on the Wednesday before the murder, she'd been approached by a man of about forty years of age, who was fairly short, pale-faced, with a black moustache. The man wore a short black coat and carried a black bag about one-foot long. He asked her to go with him but she refused. At around 2:30 a.m. on the night Mary Kelly was murdered, Sarah saw the same man in Miller's Court but managed to elude him. Just before 4 a.m. on that same morning, Lewis heard a woman shriek, "Murder!" Another woman also heard the cry but as such exclamations were commonplace and usually associated with drunken brawls or domestic violence rather than actual murder, she ignored it.

Although there are similarities to the eyewitness reports, Inspector Abberline seemed to pay most credence to the account given by Hutchinson. He even had Hutchinson walking around Whitechapel in the company of two police officers, to see if he could spot Mary's client again. Hutchinson never did. Jack the

Ripper, it seemed, had disappeared once more. Perhaps, this time, for good.

# Jack's Back

### *Rose Mylett, Alice McKenzie and Francis Coles*

Just how many women did Jack the Ripper kill? Most Ripper experts credit him with five murders, the so-called "Canonical Five" of Mary Anne Nichols, Annie Chapman, Elizabeth Stride, Catherine Eddowes, and Mary Kelly. Some, however, point to the evidence of a second man near the Stride murder scene and discount her as a Ripper victim. Still others include Stride and also Martha Tabram, killed on Tuesday, August 7, 1888, in the general vicinity of the other murders (which would make her the Ripper's first victim). And then there are those who believe that Mary Kelly was not the Ripper's last victim, that he remained active until at least 1891, sending at least three more women to a horrendous death. The victims most often mentioned in this regard are Rose Mylett, Alice McKenzie, and Francis Coles. Let us examine these cases in turn.

## Rose Mylett

At around 4:15 a.m. on the morning of December 20, 1888, Police Sergeant Robert Golding was patrolling an area known as Clarke's Yard, between 184 and 186 Poplar High Street, when he came across the body of a woman lying on the ground. Golding quickly established that the woman was not breathing, although the body was still warm. He also noticed that the position of the corpse was similar to that of the Ripper victims – lying on its left side, with the left leg drawn up and the right stretched out. However, the clothes were neither torn nor disarranged and there was no blood to suggest that she'd been the victim of a knife attack. Golding therefore drew the conclusion that this was not a Ripper murder. The pathologist's report would back up his initial assessment.

The victim was soon identified as Catherine Mylett (known to her friends as Rose). She been married to an upholsterer but had recently split from him due to her fondness for drink. Since then she had been living in various lodging houses in Whitechapel and Spitalfields and was well-known in the area as 'Drunken Lizzie.' On the night that she died, Rose was spotted in the company of two sailors at around 7:15 p.m. at which time she was reportedly sober. At around 2:30 a.m., somewhat the worse for drink, she was seen with two different men, outside The George pub in Commercial Road. It was the last time that anyone, bar her killer, saw her alive.

But was Rose Mylett really a victim of Jack the Ripper? The pathology report would suggest not. It concluded that she had been strangled to death, probably with a length of cord. In fact, there were some in the police force who believed that Mylett hadn't been murdered at all, but had choked to death after falling down drunk and catching her collar on a fence.

Not that any of that made a modicum of difference to the press, nor indeed to the public. The newspapers, of course, had a very good motive for keeping the Ripper scare alive. The Ripper sold newspapers. And so, there was widespread reportage of the murder, which all but stated that the Ripper was back. The lack of mutilation to the corpse was explained away by the assertion that Jack had probably been disturbed at his work.

As for the public, it had been five weeks since the Mary Kelly murder and the rumor mill needed feeding. It wasn't long before people were talking again in whispered tones about the Whitechapel fiend. It was almost as though they'd missed him.

## Alice McKenzie

I have yet to find anyone who has studied the Whitechapel murders and seriously considers Rose Mylett to be a Ripper victim. But what of Alice McKenzie?

On the face of it, the McKenzie murder more closely resembles the Ripper's M.O. She was found by PC Walter Andrews at around 12:50 a.m. on July 17, 1889. Andrews had been walking his beat when he spotted a woman lying on the sidewalk in Castle Alley, just off Whitechapel High Street. Closer inspection revealed two deep stab wounds to her throat, oozing blood. Additionally, her skirt had been pulled up and there was blood on her thigh and abdomen. An autopsy would later reveal that this was from a superficial wound that ran from just beneath her left breast to her belly button.

That autopsy was carried out by Dr. George Bagster Philips, the police pathologist who probably knew more about the type of mutilations carried out by the Ripper than anyone else. Having examined the victim, Phillips confidently declared that she was not a Ripper victim. The new police commissioner, James Munro, disagreed. Later that day, he penned a memo to the Home Office in which he stated that the Ripper was back. He had support in that belief from Dr. Thomas Bond and, of course, from the press.

On July 20, 1889, the East London Observer reported that:

*"The murder fiend is at his terribly ghastly work again. Countless pens are taken up again to write up the details of a mysterious and horrible crime in Whitechapel; and the heart of the nation is again harrowed by revolting stories of murder and mutilation. But what is there new to be said. Everything is on the same lines with the series of barbarous atrocities of last year - so nearly, indeed, does the crime tally with its ghastly predecessors that for all purposes we might as well tear out from the journals of that date a column or two describing one of last year's murders, alter a name here and a street there, and the sad tale would be complete."*

This report was widely inaccurate. The wounds inflicted on Alice McKenzie were not nearly as severe as those suffered by the early victims, not even Liz Stride, who had endured no postmortem mutilations. Still, the public lapped it up.

The police, meanwhile, employed their standard operating procedure in crimes of this nature. They descended on the East End en masse, working their way through the lodging houses and questioning thousands of residents. As in the past, it produced no results.

# Frances Coles

Like Alice McKenzie, Frances Coles was a prostitute. And like McKenzie, her body was discovered by a patrolling police officer in the early morning hours.

At 2:15 a.m. on the morning of Friday, November 13, 1891, PC Ernest Thompson was passing through an archway of the Great Eastern Railway, which lead from Swallow Gardens to Orman Street. Thompson had passed the spot just 15 minutes earlier and on that occasion had seen nothing out of the ordinary. Now, though, he heard footsteps walking away from him and within the shadows of the arch spotted an object lying on the ground.

Shining his lamp into the gloom, Thompson saw that it was the crumpled body of a woman and that she as quite obviously injured, with a pool of blood spreading out around her head. The policeman immediately ran to offer assistance but it didn't take him long to ascertain that the woman was beyond help. A blade had been drawn across her throat, leaving a gaping wound that ran from ear to ear.

Two blasts on Thompson's whistle brought his colleagues, PC Hyde and PC Hinton, running to the scene. They were soon joined by plainclothes officer, PC Elliott, who had been patrolling nearby Royal Mint Street. None of the officers reported seeing anyone fleeing from the scene.

PC Hyde was soon dispatched to fetch a local physician, Dr. Oxley, while PC Hinton set off for the nearest Police Station to fetch a senior officer. He returned a short while later with Inspector Flanagan in tow. Flanagan then took charge of the scene and ordered the police officers to search the immediate area and to stop and question anybody who they thought suspicious.

In accordance with a directive issued at the height of the Ripper murders, the body was left where it lay until the arrival of the Divisional Police Surgeon, Dr. George Bagster Philips. Philips duly arrived and examined the body, noting that there were two deep cuts across the throat, drawn from left to right. This, of course, was a hallmark of the Ripper's M.O. but Philips was quick to dismiss this as the work of Jack the Ripper. The posture of the body and the lack of mutilation pointed to a different perpetrator, he said.

The newspapers, however, took a different view. A report in The Times on February 14, stated that:

*"Another murder, although not so fiendish in all its details as those which were enacted within a comparatively short period of one another in Whitechapel in 1888 and 1889, has been committed in the same district, and the many similar circumstances surrounding this latest mysterious crime seem to point to its being the work of the same person. The place, the time, the character of the victim, and other points of resemblance, recall in the most obvious way the series of crimes associated in the popular mind with the so-called "Jack the Ripper."*

Other newspapers drew similar conclusions, leading to a fresh outbreak of "Ripper-mania" in the East End. The police, however, were never convinced by the theory, and in any case soon had a suspect in custody. He was James Thomas Sadler, a 53-year-old merchant seaman serving aboard the S.S. Fez. Francis Coles, it appeared, had spent the last night of her life on a pub crawl through the area with Sadler as her escort. At some point during the evening, an extremely intoxicated Sadler had been attacked by two men and a woman and robbed of his money and watch. Coles had witnessed the attack but had made no attempt to intervene, much to Sadler's disgust. The two had then argued before going their separate ways. However, Sadler had later turned up at Coles' lodging house and angrily confronted her. He was allowed by night watchman Charles Guiver, to clean up his cuts and bruises but was then asked to leave, since he had no money to pay for a bed. That was at 12:30 and a few minutes later, Frances Coles was also turned out into the night since she too was without funds.

Coles was last seen alive at 1:45 a.m. going off with a man who earlier in the evening had attacked fellow prostitute Ellen Calana on Commercial Street. Calana had tried to warn Coles about him but Coles had ignored her advice. Within hours, she'd be dead.

Thomas Sadler, meanwhile, had tried to return to his ship and become involved in an altercation with a group of dockworkers, during which he sustained another beating. He was later stopped and questioned outside an East Smithfield lodging house by Police Sergeant Edwards who let him go after Sadler stated that he had been "brutally ill-used" by a group of men at the London Docks.

With the discovery of Frances Coles' body and the various reports putting Sadler in her company on the night of her death, a warrant was issued. Sadler was traced to the Phoenix beer house and promptly arrested.

But the case against Sadler was an exceedingly weak one and it would eventually collapse after he was able to prove that he was not with Coles in the hours before she died. His eventual acquittal saw him cheered from the courtroom.

So James Sadler was not the killer of Francis Coles and most certainly not Jack the Ripper. But what of the violent punter who Ellen Calana tried to warn Francis about. It seems an even bet that this man was responsible for the Coles murder, but was he Jack? The evidence suggests not. Had he been Jack the Ripper it is unlikely that Ellen Calana would have survived to tell her tale.

# Part 2:
# Who Was Jack the Ripper?

# The Usual Suspects

*And Why None of Them Is Jack the Ripper*

No case of serial murder in history has thrown up as many suspects as that of Jack the Ripper. Over time, the list has grown to over 100 names, ranging from the ludicrous (Prince Albert Victor, Lewis Carroll) to the unlikely (Francis Tumblety, George Chapman) to the impossible (Michael Ostrog, Walter Sickert).

Some of these suspects were named by senior officers who worked the case but many more have been the dredged up by authors putting out books that offer pet theories on the Ripper's identity. Inevitably, in these cases, the facts are manipulated to fit the hypothesis. As a result, most of these theories are easy to disprove.

I believe that the opposite approach is far more useful. Begin with what we know about the case and see how the suspect measures up against that criteria. Any candidate that does not match up to the known facts can then safely be disregarded.

With that in mind, let's begin with the contemporary suspects, those named by senior police officers with close ties to the case.

## Montague John Druitt

The favorite suspect of Sir Melville Macnaghten, Druitt was a 31-year-old barrister who supplemented his income by working as an assistant schoolteacher at a school in Blackheath. Macnaghten's primary evidence appears to have been that Druitt was thought to be sexually insane and that his own family believed him to be the Ripper. Druitt disappeared three weeks after the murder of Mary Kelly and his body was pulled from the Thames on December 31, 1888. The jury at the inquest returned a verdict of suicide by drowning "whilst of unsound mind." Macnaghten took this to mean that the horrendous injuries inflicted on Mary Kelly had finally driven Druitt over the edge. It also conveniently explained why the murders stopped after the Miller's Court atrocity.

*Montague John Druitt*

On the face of it, Druitt makes a strong candidate, but when we look more closely at Macnaghten's "evidence" a number of gaping holes appear. For starters, Macnaghten's information did not come directly from the Druitt family but from an unnamed third party. And the information was far from accurate. For example, Macnaghten stated in a memorandum that Druitt was 41 years old and that he was a doctor. Neither of these is correct.

Ripper experts have also noted that Druitt was a poor physical fit for Jack. While he was of medium height, he was slightly built, quite unlike the stocky man described at the crime scenes. He also lived some distance away, in Blackheath, and was not known to frequent the East End. And if that is not reason enough to doubt, Druitt had a cast-iron alibi for at least one of the murders (Annie Chapman).

Nonetheless, the timing of Druitt's death, coinciding as it did with the last of the Whitechapel murders, marked him out as a suspect. Police Commissioner Sir Charles Warren was known to consider him the most viable suspect. However, the most knowledgeable man on the Whitechapel murders, Chief Inspector Abberline, did not believe Druitt was the Ripper.

## Aaron Kosminski

Another suspect mentioned by Macnaghten, and also by Assistant Commissioner Sir Robert Anderson and Chief Inspector Donald Swanson, was a man named Aaron Kosminski. According to Macnaghten, Kosminski was a Polish Jew, resident in Whitechapel. "This man became insane owing to many years' indulgence in solitary vices," MacNaghten noted. "He had a great hatred of women, especially of the prostitute class, and had strong homicidal tendencies; he was removed to a lunatic asylum about March 1889."

Sir Robert Anderson also references Kosminski, in his memoirs, written in 1910. Although Anderson doesn't offer a name, it is clear from his description that he was referring to Kosminski. He even hints that the police knew that Kosminski was the Ripper but lacked the evidence to arrest him.

Anderson wrote: "Undiscovered murders are rare in London, and the 'Jack the Ripper' crimes are not in that category. I will merely add that the only person who ever had a good view of the murderer unhesitatingly identified the suspect the instant he was confronted with him; but he refused to give evidence against him. In saying that he was a Polish Jew I am merely stating a definitely ascertained fact."

Swanson takes this even further. He tells us that the eyewitness was a Jew and refused to testify because the suspect was also of that faith and he did not want the man's death (by hanging) to be on his conscience. He goes on to state that the suspect was placed under surveillance after the Mary Kelly murder but was shortly thereafter committed to Colney Hatch lunatic asylum where he died a short while later. He ends with the emphatic statement, "Kosminski was the suspect."

So who was Aaron Kosminski? It appears that he genuinely was insane, paranoid, delusional, most likely a schizophrenic. He claimed to hear voices and to receive instructions from a higher power that informed him of the movements of all mankind.

Another of his many quirks was that he refused to eat anything other than food he picked up out of the gutter.

But there are many arguments against Aaron Kosminski as Jack the Ripper. Firstly, the information given as fact by Chief Inspector Swanson is largely inaccurate. Kosminski was not removed to an asylum in March 1889, as stated, but sometime in 1891. And he did not die soon afterwards, he remained incarcerated for another 25 years during which time he was described as a "harmless imbecile."

Are we to believe that the Ripper, having committed five extraordinary murders in just three months, would then suddenly lay dormant for two whole years before his incarceration? Highly unlikely.

And Kosminski, short and slight of frame, did not match eyewitness descriptions either, neither did he possess any medical skill. Aside from that, the Ripper's M.O. does not support the theory of a psychotic killer. Jack was able to carry out quite specific mutilations under extreme pressure, hardly something you'd associate with the imbecilic Kosminski.

## Michael Ostrog

A petty thief and confidence trickster, Ostrog spent most of his adult life in prison. Macnaghten described him as, "a Russian doctor, and a convict who was subsequently detained in a lunatic asylum as a homicidal maniac. This man's antecedents were of the worst possible type, and his whereabouts at the time of the murders could never be ascertained."

But as with Macnaghten's assessments of the previous two suspects, this is simply not true. Ostrog was not a doctor, although he sometimes posed as one to carry out his scams. He was also not a "homicidal maniac." In fact, despite an extensive arrest record, he was never picked up for any violent act.

*Michael Ostrog*

Quite aside from that, Ostrog is perhaps the least likely candidate of the original suspects. At 60, he was way too old and, at 5-foot-11, he was much too tall.  The only thing that may have pointed to him as a suspect was that his whereabouts during the three months that the Ripper committed his atrocities were unknown, and that Ostrog lied about them under questioning. That lie, as it turns out, comprehensively rules Ostrog out as a suspect. During the time of the Ripper murders, he was languishing in a French prison.

## Francis Tumbelty

Tumbelty's name first entered the annals of Ripperology courtesy of a letter written by Chief Inspector John Littlechild to the journalist George Sims in 1913. In it, Littlechild proffered the name Tumblety as a Ripper suspect, also stating that Tumbelty was "an American quack" who was "arrested for an unnatural act" and subsequently "committed suicide at the time the Ripper murders came to an end."

At least some of Littlechild's assertions are accurate. Tumblety was indeed an American who made his living peddling quack medicines. And he had been arrested for "gross indecency," although the offenses he was accused of tend to cast doubt on his candidacy as Jack the Ripper. The charges related to indecent acts with men. Homosexual serial killers, as we now know, seek out male victims, making it highly unlikely that Tumblety (if he was a killer at all) would have attacked women.

Furthermore, Tumbelty was too old to have been Jack and, at six-foot, he was too tall. He also had no medical training, despite referring to himself as a doctor. And Littlechild was also wrong about Tumbelty's suicide. He did not kill himself but rather skipped bail on the indecency charge and fled to France. He later returned to America.

## George Chapman (real name: Severin Antoniovich Klosowski)

As the suspect favored by Chief Inspector Abberline, George Chapman warrants serious consideration. He certainly ticks many of the boxes. He was apprenticed to a surgeon while living in his native Poland; he moved to London 18 months before the murders started and was living in Whitechapel for their duration; he was known to be violent towards women and would eventually be hanged for poisoning three of his wives; he was single at the time of the Whitechapel murders and therefore free to roam the streets at all hours; he worked a regular job which meant he was occupied during the week but free on weekends.

*Severin Klosowski a.k.a. George Chapman*

However, there are also many reasons to question his candidacy. One is age; Chapman was 23 years old in 1888, younger than the man seen by witnesses. Eyewitnesses accounts are often unreliable though, and Chapman may simply have looked older than his years. But even if we overlook age, we encounter another problem when we consider why a man who'd savagely murdered five women in the space of just three months would suddenly stop. Chapman remained in London for two more years after the Ripper murders before immigrating to America in 1891 (he'd return to England just a year later). So if he was Jack the Ripper, why did he suddenly stop killing?

But perhaps the most significant reason for questioning George Chapman's inclusion as a Ripper suspect is the difference between the Ripper murders and the crimes for which he was eventually hanged, the poisoning deaths of three women. Is it possible to reconcile the homicidal maniac, Jack the Ripper, with the coolly, calculating poisoner, George Chapman? Inspector Abberline seemed to think so, but he was working without the wealth of knowledge we now have about serial killers. Suffice to say that if George Chapman and Jack the Ripper were one and the same person, the change in modus operandi would be without precedent.

## Thomas Cutbush

Whether or not Thomas Cutbush had anything to do with the Whitechapel murders (the evidence suggests not), he certainly has made a significant contribution to Ripper folklore.

In 1894, an editorial appeared in the Sun newspaper suggesting Cutbush as a suspect (although not naming him). After reading the article, Sir Melville Macnaghten decided to compose his now famous memorandum, which named three candidates he considered more likely than Cutbush (Druitt, Kosminski, and Ostrog). In that same document, Macnaghten stated emphatically that the Ripper had only murdered five women, thus giving us the "Canonical Five."

But who was Thomas Cutbush, and why was he considered a possible Jack the Ripper? The main accusation against Cutbush appears to be that he had contracted syphilis from a prostitute and was driven insane, leading to a thirst for revenge. This assertion, however, has been proven false. Cutbush's admission record to Broadmoor asylum in 1891 makes no mention of venereal disease and states rather that his affliction was hereditary.

There are several other reasons to disregard Cutbush. He was a slightly built man, quite unlike the individual described by eyewitnesses. And while he was most certainly violent, he was also described as: "Dirty, destructive, degraded and demented. An imbecile." This hardly portrays a man who was able to talk a prostitute into a dark alley and then to kill her silently, carry out specific mutilations, and walk calmly from the scene without being noticed.

## More Recent Theories

### David Cohen

In an article published in Psychology Today in January 2014, Dr. Scott Bonn identifies a man named David Cohen as Jack the Ripper. According to Bonn, Cohen was a poor Polish Jew with homicidal tendencies who was admitted to Colney Hatch Lunatic Asylum in December 1888 and died there ten months later in October 1889.

In support of this theory, Bonn cites the autopsy reports compiled by Dr. George Bagster Phillips and Dr. Thomas Bond at the time of the murders, as well as speculations made by Bond as to the Ripper's likely character ("a man of solitary habits, subject to periodic attacks of homicidal and erotic mania, and the character of the mutilations possibly indicating "satyriasis" or uncontrollable sexual desire). Bonn then fortifies this opinion by drawing on the behavioral profile of Jack the Ripper compiled by FBI Special Agent John Douglas.

Bonn also states emphatically that the Ripper had no knowledge of anatomy, once again citing the opinion of Dr. Bond, but conveniently ignoring that of every other pathologist involved in the case, including Dr. Bagster Phillips. Dr. Phillips was convinced that Jack had at least some medical training. Incidentally, the FBI profile draws a similar conclusion.

Another problem with Bonn's suspect is that he describes him as "violent, destructive, and non-communicative." These, Bonn says, are the typical characteristics of a disorganized serial killer, of which Jack was one.

The thing is, serial killers are seldom entirely organized or entirely disorganized and Jack the Ripper certainly showed characteristics of both types. The victims may have been chosen at random and the bodies left where they fell. But there is also evidence to suggest that Jack engaged the women in conversation and coaxed them to isolated areas. These are behaviors typically associated with organized serial killers.

Finally, the name "David Cohen" does not refer to a specific person but was rather a "John Doe" type name applied to Jewish inmates whose identities could not be established (in fairness, Bonn admits as much in his article).

So essentially, what Bonn is saying is that Jack the Ripper was a Polish Jew inmate with supposed homicidal tendencies who was admitted to Colney Hatch Lunatic Asylum early in 1889. Supposedly, only one person matching that description was admitted to Colney Hatch during the period 1888 to 1890. But does that necessarily mean that that person was Jack the Ripper? It would take a massive leap of faith to draw such a conclusion.

## Carl Feigenbaum

Carl Ferdinand Feigenbaum was first mentioned in connection with the Whitechapel murders in 1896. A merchant seaman of German descent, Feigenbaum was arrested in New York City in 1895, for cutting a woman's throat and was subsequently executed for the crime. After the execution, his lawyer, William Sanford Lawton, claimed that Feigenbaum had admitted to having a pathological hatred of women and a desire to kill and mutilate them. Lawton went one step further, stating that he believed Feigenbaum to be Jack the Ripper.

Although the idea received some press coverage at the time, no one seriously considered Feigenbaum a viable suspect until author Trevor Marriott revived the idea over a century later. Marriott, a former British homicide investigator, posited the theory that Feigenbaum had committed the Whitechapel murders as well as

Ripper-like killings in the United States and Germany between 1891 and 1894. However, other researchers have pointed out that some of the murders that Marriott attributed to Feigenham did not actually happen but were, in fact, newspaper fabrications designed to boost circulation.

Whether that is true or not, there is no evidence that places Feigenbaum in Whitechapel at the time of the Ripper murders. Marriott's theory, that Feigenbaum might have traveled to and from London during the autumn of 1888, committing murders during each stopover, is plausible, but it hardly amounts to proof.

## Crackpot Theories

Whatever the merits (or otherwise) of the theories presented above, one can at least understand some logical reason behind them. The same cannot be said for some of the other suspects offered up over the years, ranging from the ridiculous to the outright bizarre.

### Prince Albert Victor

Prince Albert Victor was Queen Victoria's grandson and heir to the British throne. This ludicrous theory hinges on the Prince fathering a child by an East End prostitute and then concocting a plot to get rid of the child's mother and all of her prostitute friends who knew of his indiscretion. Various sub-theories have Sir William Gull, the royal physician, as the Ripper, acting under orders from Queen Victoria herself. This idea originated in Stephen Knight's 1974 bestseller, "Jack the Ripper: The Final

Solution." Subsequent film adaptations include, "Murder by Decree" (1978) and "From Hell" (2008).

Even if we take this theory seriously, it is a matter of record that Prince Albert was in Scotland when some of the murders were committed. As for Gull, he was 70 years old at the time of the murders and had recently suffered a stroke.

## Walter Sickert

Almost as ridiculous is the notion, proffered by best-selling author Patricia Cornwell, that renowned English painter, Walter Sickert was the Ripper. Cornwell's theory is based primarily on the belief that some of Sickert's paintings (completed 20 years after the event) resemble the Ripper crime scenes.

Cornwall cites Sickert's impotence, leading to a deep-set hatred of women, as his prime motive. But Sickert's first wife divorced him for infidelity and it was common knowledge that he maintained several mistresses, making a mockery of this assertion. Additionally, Sickert was in France when most of the murders occurred.

## Lewis Carroll

This one has renowned author Lewis Carroll as the Ripper with clues about the murders inserted into his most famous work, Alice in Wonderland. The idea was first put forward by author Richard

Wallace in his book "Jack the Ripper, Light-Hearted Friend." It is rightly ridiculed by serious scholars of the case.

## Jill the Ripper

Another outlandish notion states that the Ripper was actually a woman. Bizarre though this theory sounds, it was first postulated by Inspector Abbeline himself. Abberline thought that it might explain how the killer could have escaped from the crime scenes so effortlessly.

Later, Aberline ran the idea past Dr. Thomas Dutton, who said that it was unlikely, but that if the killer were a woman she would most probably be a midwife. Thus, the legend of Jill the Ripper was born. Today, you'd be hard pressed to find anyone who takes the idea seriously.

## James Maybrick

Not so much a ridiculous theory as a proven hoax. In 1992, a Liverpool scrap metal dealer, Michael Barrett, claimed to have found the diary of a cotton broker named James Maybrick, who died in 1889. In the journal, Maybrick confesses to being Jack the Ripper.

The document provoked huge excitement and earned Barrett a book deal with Smith Gryphon Ltd, with the subsequent release proving a runaway bestseller. However, the diary was subsequently found to be a forgery, and Barrett eventually admitted to the deception.

# Ripper Myths Debunked

*Jack the Ripper in Fact and Fiction*

As well as a veritable boatload of suspects, the Ripper murders have been the source of all manner of myths and legends. Some of these hark back to the original inquiry and to statements made by investigators and pathologists (often erroneously). Others have their genesis in "factual" books on the case and to authors gleefully bending the facts in order to fit them to their pet theories. In this section, we will examine some of the most prevalent Ripper myths and hopefully set the record straight once and for all.

## Myth # 1: The Ripper was a Doctor

One of the most controversial aspects of the case centers around the Ripper's supposed anatomical knowledge. Was Jack a medical man? The simple answer is that we don't know. But that doesn't mean that we can't venture an educated guess, based on the available evidence.

First up, there is the opinion of the surgeons who examined the bodies. Almost all of these agreed that the killer possessed some anatomical knowledge and surgical skill. The main dissenting voice was that of Dr. Thomas Bond, who insisted that the Ripper possessed no skill at all, not even that of a horse slaughter.

But does Dr. Bond's assertion stand up to the known evidence? Consider the conditions under which the Ripper had to work – outdoors, often in near total darkness, under extremely tight time constraints, and with the ever-present threat of discovery. Now consider the fact that he was able to remove the kidney of one victim and the uterus of another, both without damaging the surrounding organs. Considering these factors, it seems almost certain that the Ripper knew where and how to cut. That knowledge could only have come through some form of medical training.

That said, it is unlikely that Jack was a qualified medical doctor. If we accept, as most experts do, that he lived in the East End, and if we accept also that the police will have been aware of all practicing physicians living in the area, it seems impossible that he could have evaded detection.

So where does that leave us? The FBI profile compiled by Supervisory Special Agent John Douglas suggests that he may have been a mortician's helper, hospital attendant, or medical examiner's assistant. There are also suggestions that he may have worked as a butcher, perhaps one with a keen interest in human anatomy.

Of course, we don't know that he wasn't a doctor. Perhaps a foreign national who had practiced medicine in his home country but was unable to obtain the necessary accreditation in Britain.

## Myth # 2: The Ripper was Left-handed

All of the evidence suggests otherwise and yet this belief persists. It probably harks back to the Polly Nichols murder. Dr. Rees Llewellyn, the first doctor to examine the body, initially stated his opinion that the killer was left-handed although he later amended that statement and said that he wasn't sure. Other surgeons involved in the case believed that Jack was either right-handed or ambidextrous.

So what does the evidence tell us? The cuts inflicted on the victims' throats all ran from left to right and were made by someone who was standing to the right of the victim as she lay on the ground. The reason that the killer positioned himself thus is obvious. He wanted to avoid the spurt of arterial blood as the throat was cut. It would have been unnatural for a left-handed person to adopt such a position.

There is other evidence too, to suggest that Jack was right-handed. Polly Nichols, Annie Chapman, and Catherine Eddowes were all position with a barrier (a wall or a fence) to their left. That places the killer to the right of the body and as we have already observed, this is an awkward position for a left-hander to operate from. Jack the Ripper was definitely not left-handed.

## Myth # 3: The Ripper had an Accomplice

Although most Ripper experts are convinced that Jack operated alone, there are some who believe that he had an accomplice, perhaps someone who acted as a lookout. Support for this theory comes from the murder of Elizabeth Stride and the evidence given by eyewitness Israel Schwartz.

According to Schwartz, he was walking along Berner Street in the direction of the International Working Men's Educational Club, when he spotted a man and a woman involved in a tussle. Not wanting to get involved, he crossed the road, but as he did, spotted a second man, standing in the shadows, lighting his pipe. As Schwartz passed him, the man who was attacking the woman called out to this second man, "Lipski!" The second man then started following Schwartz, causing him to panic and run.

Schwartz would later relate this story to both the police and the press, but as his version seemed to change with each retelling, the police all but dismissed it. Were they right to do so? After all, what reason was there for Schwartz to have concocted such a fanciful tale? The likelihood is that he was telling the truth about what he saw.

But does that mean that the second man was somehow involved in the crime? Probably not. A more feasible answer is that Schwartz simply misread the situation. "Lipski!" was a common taunt directed at Jews in those days and it is likely that the attacker was talking to Schwartz when he said it, not to the second man. In his panicked state, Schwartz is also likely to have misconstrued the second man's actions. The man was not following him, simply heading in the same direction (and probably also making haste to avoid the altercation going on across the road). In any case, Chief Inspector Swanson later revealed that the "second man" had been traced and cleared him of any involvement in Elizabeth Stride's murder. Jack the Ripper almost certainly worked alone.

## Myth # 4: The Murders Were Committed as Part of a Conspiracy

This idea owes its genesis to a 1973 BBC documentary and to Stephen Knight's adaptation of the theories presented therein. Knight's book "Jack the Ripper: The Final Solution," and its subsequent film adaptations, "Murder by Decree" and "From Hell," posited the quite ridiculous idea that the Whitechapel murders were committed in order to cover up a scandal involving Queen Victoria's grandson, and heir to the British throne, Prince Albert Victor.

Knight's theory goes something like this. The prince, while slumming it in the East End disguised as a commoner, met a girl named Annie Elizabeth Crook in a tobacconist's shop in Cleveland Street. Instantly smitten, the prince started a relationship with the girl and soon got her pregnant. When word of this reached the ears of Queen Victoria, she was furious and demanded that the situation be handled at once. Marriage, of course, was out of the question, since Annie was not only a commoner, but a Catholic.

Queen Victoria thus called in her Prime Minister, Robert Gascoyne-Cecil and tasked him with resolving the issue. Cecil, in turn, called on Sir William Gull, the Queen's personal physician who ordered that Annie be taken into custody and whisked away to a secret location. There, experiments were performed on her in an attempt to eradicate all memory of her relationship with the Prince. As a result, she went insane and was subsequently released.

Enter Walter Sickert, the renowned English artist and a sometime Ripper suspect himself. Sickert was a friend of the Prince and he took pity on Annie and decided to hire a nurse to care for her. That nurse was Mary Kelly, later to become the Ripper's final victim.

It all might have ended there had Kelly not fallen on hard times and taken to drink and prostitution. Then, she started shooting her mouth off about the secrets she knew. Most people ignored her pronouncements as drunken ranting but a group of her friends - Polly Nichols, Liz Stride, and Annie Chapman - convinced her to start blackmailing the government. When Cecil heard of the threat, he called on Gull once again.

Gull then devised a plan to get rid of the troublesome whores and kill off the scandal once and for all. He recruited a coachman named John Netley and started murdering the women one by one. The murder of Catherine Eddowes had been a case of mistaken identity as she often went by the alias Mary Kelly. Even police commissioner Sir Robert Anderson is drawn into the conspiracy, tasked with ensuring that the murders were never solved.

There is more to this quite ludicrous theory, including a subplot to implicate each of the most commonly mentioned Ripper suspects. It all makes for great fiction but there is very little evidence to support it. Simply put, there was no royal conspiracy.

## Myth # 5: The Police Were Incompetent

One of the most widespread misconceptions about the case is that the Ripper escaped justice due to police ineptitude. This is simply not true. The police of the day did everything that was humanly possible to catch the Ripper given the constraints of technology and resources that they were up against. That the Ripper escaped detection is as much down to dumb luck as to police ineptitude or the stealth of the killer.

The police, in truth, started out with the deck stacked significantly against them. The Whitechapel murders were unlike anything they'd ever been confronted with before, the random murder of strangers. And they were ill-equipped to deal with such a series of crimes. Modern investigative techniques like offender profiling and DNA testing were, of course, not available. Fingerprinting was still in its infancy and looked upon with suspicion by senior law enforcement officers.

The terrain also favored the Ripper. Whitechapel and Spitalfields were a bewildering maze of alleyways, yards, and narrow streets, ill-lit and masked in shadow. If, as is commonly believed, the Ripper was a local, he'd have had a significant advantage over his pursuers. It also helped that his victims went so willingly with him to dark and secluded places.

Then there was the sheer volume of evidence generated by the case. The Metropolitan Police Force of that era was woefully undermanned and they were quickly overwhelmed by the number of tips and suggestions that came in. Not all of these were well intentioned. The number of crank letters alone amounted to several hundred, each of which had to be checked out. In addition, the police carried out thousands of interviews and searched dozens of lodging houses in the area.

If there is any criticism that can be levied at the police, it is perhaps the lack of imagination shown by those in charge. Clearly, this was a new type of crime and perhaps needed a fresh approach. Yet the police persisted in their tried and tested methods of curfews, searches, and leaning on informants. They failed, for example, to employ the fledgling technology of fingerprinting, they failed to make adequate use of the press, they failed to convince the Home Secretary to agree to a reward for information.

Still, it is hard to be too harsh on the police. Even with modern technology, stranger killers are notoriously difficult to apprehend, prostitute slayers even more so. The Metropolitan Police were not incompetent. Jack had the luck of the devil.

## Myth # 6: Jack the Ripper Wrote the Goulston Street Graffito

The infamous "writing on the wall" has been quoted by many sources as a missed opportunity to catch the Ripper. But was it really? Just to recap, we are referring here to the cryptic message scrawled on a wall in Goulston Street on the night of the "double event."

"The Juwes are the men that will not be blamed for nothing," it read, in an apparent boast by a Jewish killer about his crimes. The main reason that it was associated with the Ripper was that a bloodstained piece of Catherine Eddowes' apron was found nearby. The theory is that while fleeing the crime scene, the Ripper had stopped long enough to chalk his taunting message, dropping the scrap of fabric in the process.

But did he really? Does it really seem feasible that the Ripper would expose himself to the possibility of capture simply to taunt the police? Jack had shown himself to be a pretty cool customer in the commission of his crimes, but why take such an outrageous risk for so scant a reward?

The truth is that Jack was not the author of the Goulston Graffito and the message likely had nothing to do with the case. He did indeed pass that way, dropping the strip of apron as he did. Perhaps he saw the message and was thereby inspired to create controversy by dropping the clue nearby, perhaps the scrap of fabric just landed fortuitously.

No photographic record of the message survives, of course. It was obliterated on the instruction of Police Commissioner Sir Charles Warren when he arrived to inspect the site at 5:30 a.m. However, those who saw the message said that it was slightly smudged and had obviously been there for some time. Jack the Ripper, in other words, had nothing to do with it.

## Myth # 7: The Ripper Sent Taunting Letters to the Police

The Ripper letters are as much a part of the case as the murders themselves but as far as can be established they were not penned by Jack but by various hoaxers. And the most famous of the more than 300 missives claiming to be from Jack the Ripper were not addressed to the authorities at all. The "Dear Boss" letter, which gave the killer his infamous nom de guerre, was addressed to the Central News Agency, while the "From Hell" letter, which accompanied a parcel containing half a human kidney, was sent to Mr. George Lusk, Chairman of the Mile End Vigilance Committee.

So if Jack himself did not write the letters, who did? As far as can be established, the "Dear Boss" letter (and another that followed it) was penned by a journalist by the name of Thomas J. Bulling, who worked for the Central News Agency. Bulling's motive was obvious. Ripper stories sold newspapers and the boastful, threatening tone of the missive struck just the right note with readers. Despite the police immediately dismissing the letter as a hoax, the public perception was that it was real. That belief persisted for decades.

The other letter is slightly more problematic as the author has never been named. It also contained the chunk of kidney which the author claimed was from Ripper victim, Catherine Eddowes. That claim was never verified one way or another but it entered Ripper legend as fact, mainly due to the press vastly misrepresenting a report compiled by Dr. Thomas Openshaw, Pathological Curator of London Hospital.

All that Openshaw would confirm was that the kidney was probably human. However, according to the stories run by the tabloids, he had also stated that it was from a woman of around 45 years of age, recently deceased, and a heavy gin drinker. In other words, it was a perfect match for Catherine Eddowes. A story that later circulated held that the kidney showed signs of Bright's disease, which Eddowes apparently suffered from. None of this is true. All of the doctors who examined the kidney believed that it was not from Eddowes and was probably part of a prank perpetrated by a medical student.

## Myth # 8: Jack the Ripper Committed Suicide

Since we don't know the identity of Jack the Ripper, it is impossible to determine how he met his end or indeed why he suddenly stopped killing. There are a couple of possibilities. The Ripper may have been arrested for an unrelated crime and thrown into prison, he may have been committed to an insane asylum, he may have left the area or even the country, he may have died of disease or been killed. He may even have stopped killing of his own volition, although given the extreme violence of his crimes and the short "cooling off" period between them, this is unlikely.

Another possibility is that he committed suicide. In fact, one of the most oft- mentioned Ripper suspects, Montague John Druitt, met his end in just that way, with his timely demise presented as the reason for the cessation of the murders. Druitt, of course, was not Jack the Ripper. We know that much for certain.

But how likely is it that the real Ripper took his own life? Most unlikely, indeed. Everything we know about this type of killer informs us that he does not commit suicide.

Serial killers, in the main, are psychopaths and therefore without empathy or compassion. They feel no guilt over their acts. And that personality trait discounts the most popular motive presented for the Ripper suicide theory – that he was so traumatized by the havoc he wreaked on Mary Kelly's body that he took his own life. This does not gel with what we know.

In all my years of writing about and researching the subject, the only serial killer suicides I have encountered occurred while the killer was in custody (e.g. Fred West, Harold Shipman) or placed in a hopeless situation where arrest was imminent (e.g. Herb Baumeister, Leonard Lake). Neither of these situations applied to Jack. It is safe to assume that Jack the Ripper did not kill himself.

## Myth # 9: Jack the Ripper was Insane

The Whitechapel murders presented an entirely new challenge to the police force of the day, one that they were ill-equipped to deal with. Murder in the East End at the time was not uncommon, but it was certainly no more prevalent than in other areas of London. And murders of this type, the slaying of complete strangers for no apparent reason, were unheard of. The only inference that the public, the press, and indeed the police could draw was that the killer must be a raving lunatic. One major focus of the investigation, in fact, was to trawl the records of London asylums for violent lunatics currently at large. Many of these men were arrested and interrogated. All were cleared.

The police, of course, were barking up the wrong tree with this line of inquiry. What we know now about serial killers tells us that they are outwardly normal, even personable individuals, who attract very little attention to themselves. Eyewitness reports suggest that Jack was able to approach his victims and engage them in conversation. He was even able to lure them to dark and isolated spots.

There is also strong circumstantial evidence to suggest that Jack was in regular employment. The murders all occurred on weekends or bank holidays, suggesting that these were the days on which he could afford to be prowling the streets in the early morning hours. It is also likely that he lived locally, in close proximity to other people. At a time when suspicion and angst over the murders ran at fever pitch, any unusual behavior would surely have been reported to the police.

We must therefore assume that Jack was able to present himself as entirely normal to those around him. There can be little doubt that he was a psychopath but he was not psychotic.

## Myth # 10: The Ripper was a Myth. He Never Really Existed

This is perhaps the granddaddy of all Ripper myths, that the Ripper never existed, that the crimes were random acts of violence perpetrated by different offenders, that the whole thing was a massive hoax dreamed up by the newspapers to improve circulation.

The question we need to ask ourselves is whether this is possible and the obvious answer is, yes it is. The possibility that five separate perpetrators murdered five different women within an area of less than a mile cannot be ruled out. But is it likely? The answer to that question is, emphatically, no.

Modern day investigators have learned how to link individual murders together by looking for the killer's "signature." Contrary to popular belief, a serial killer's modus operandi does not remain consistent over time. It almost always evolves, with the killer learning with each new crime. What does not evolve is the killer's "signature."

These are ritualistic behaviors performed at the crime scene almost without thinking. They are the product of the killer's fantasy life; elements he will have gone over hundreds of times in his mind long before crossing the threshold to actual murder. As such, they are buried deep within his psyche and nigh on impossible to fake, even by a copycat killer.

In the Ripper's case, the signature is clear and unambiguous in all of the five canonical murders. The victims were brought under control quickly by strangulation and then swiftly dispatched by a couple of slashes to the throat. As mentioned elsewhere in this book, the method was always the same, the victim on her back, the knife drawn from left to right with the killer positioned to the right of the victim to avoid the spray of blood. There was no hesitation, no trial cuts. Mutilations were targeted mainly at the abdomen and, although horrendous, were inflicted on a corpse rather than a living victim.

This actually tells us quite a lot about the Ripper's motivations and personality (to be examined further in the next chapters). More importantly, in the context of the question being addressed, it tells us that the same man was responsible for at least four of the five canonical victims (the possible exception is Liz Stride). It is ludicrous to suggest that five killers, working independently of each other, could have committed five murders with such a consistent signature.

The only conclusion we can draw is that Jack the Ripper was very real and that he killed at least five women and quite possibly more than that.

# The Profilers

## *A Modern Take on Jack the Ripper*

It is an intriguing question. Would a modern police force, equipped with current technology, have caught the Ripper? The natural inclination is to answer with an emphatic "yes." And if you throw in current surveillance technology, then you may well be right. The possibility of a single killer getting away with five high profile murders, in such a constrained area, within such a short time-frame, is perhaps unlikely in the modern day.

But, as most homicide investigators will tell you, catching a serial killer is no easy task. The decades-long hunts for the Green River Killer and the BTK Killer provide ample illustration of that fact. Still, it is tempting to imagine a team of Cold Case detectives pouring over the Ripper case files and unearthing some scrap of evidence that all who had come before had somehow missed, some scrap of evidence that unmasks the Ripper at last.

Unfortunately, that is not going to happen. Investigative techniques in the late 1800's were remarkably crude and involved very little by way of physical evidence collection. No fiber evidence was collected, no blood or other fluids, no fingerprints. In most cases, crime scene photographs were not even taken. Autopsies performed on the victims were likewise cursory, the notes somewhat cryptic by today's standards.

Yet imperfect though these sources were, they might have provided our fictional Cold Case team with some basis for examination. That is, if we still had all of the original police files. Unfortunately, we do not. Many have been destroyed over the years, some during the Second World War blitz on London, some due to poor record keeping or deliberate destruction to make space for newer case files. It all leaves Ripper researchers in the frustrating position of having to fill in the gaps from secondary sources. These sources, of course, are usually subjective, leading to various untruths and misconceptions bleeding into Ripper lore over the years.

One field of investigative protocol that has been applied to the case is that of Offender Profiling. Although generally considered a modern technique, this discipline has been in use, in one form of another, since the Middle Ages. In fact, Dr. Thomas Bond was asked to prepare a profile of sorts during the original Ripper investigation. Dr. Bond was asked specifically to determine whether the Ripper had any medical expertise. (Bond concluded that the Ripper did not have medical training, although most experts disagree with him).

Antecedents aside, the field of Offender Profiling first achieved widespread recognition through its use by the FBI's Behavioral Science Unit. One of the technology's foremost practitioners is former Supervisory Special Agent John Douglas. In 1988, the 100th anniversary of the Whitechapel Murders, Douglas was asked to prepare a criminal profile of Jack the Ripper. His findings make for interesting reading.

According to Douglas, Jack the Ripper was the product of a home in which the mother was the domineering individual, the father being either a weakling or altogether absent. Jack's mother was a heavy drinker and a promiscuous individual, something which left the boy with a simmering anger. He responded by becoming withdrawn and taking out his frustrations on animals. He was probably also a fire starter.

As a young adult, Jack remained a loner. In lieu of human contact, he developed a rich fantasy life, which grew to include fantasies of murdering and mutilating women. None of this would have been apparent to the people around him.

Jack would have pursued a profession that required minimal interaction with people. He may have been a butcher and slaughter or perhaps a hospital worker or mortician's assistant. He would have been quiet and somewhat shy in the presence of others and an obsessively neat dresser. Socially inadequate, his experience with the opposite sex would have been limited. His sexual needs will have been serviced through encounters with prostitutes, even though they would have reviled him. He may have contracted a sexually transmitted disease through these encounters, further fueling his hatred of women in general and prostitutes in particular.

Like most Ripper experts, Douglas is of the opinion that Jack lived in the East End and that the first murder was committed close to his home or place of work. The murders would have been unplanned, the victims chosen at random. Douglas believes that Jack routinely carried a knife for protection. The nights on which he killed probably started with him drinking at his local pub. Alcohol would have lowered his inhibitions and he'd then have hit the streets, wandering aimlessly until he encountered some unfortunate victim. He'd have likely passed up many opportunities before finding a victim who could be killed without risking discovery.

Another interesting idea put forward by Douglas was that the Ripper might have dressed up before going out hunting for prostitutes, wearing his best suit to create the impression that he was a man of some means. This might explain the description given by Elizabeth Long of the man seen talking to Annie Chapman. She described him as "shabby genteel."

Douglas also addresses some common Ripper myths in his profile. He discounts emphatically the theory that the killer might have been a woman. He also dismisses the idea that Jack committed suicide. He thinks it unlikely that Jack would have stopped killing on his own and thinks it more likely that he was arrested and incarcerated for some other crime.

Another famous profiler to take on the job of assessing Jack the Ripper is Professor David Canter of the University of Surrey. Professor Canter is Britain's most renowned profiler and has produced some astoundingly accurate summations, most notably of "Railway Killer" John Duffy.

Canter's assessment agrees with Douglas on many points but offers that the Ripper may have been married at some point, although the relationship would have been strained. He also suggests that the Ripper would have been suffering from some psychological problem of which those closest to him would have been aware. Canter's Ripper is not quite so much of an introvert as the man described by Douglas. He may have had a job that required limited social interaction since he was adept at engaging prostitutes in conversation and putting them at ease.

One point on which Douglas and Canter agree is that the Ripper would have committed other crimes before making the step up to murder. He might well have had a police record for rape, robbery or assault in the years prior to the commencement of the Whitechapel murders. This is common among serial killers and might well be an avenue to explore for those who seek the identity of Jack the Ripper.

# Examining the Evidence

*What do we really know about Saucy Jack?*

Let's be blunt about this. Barring some startling new discovery, it is highly unlikely that we will ever know the Ripper's identity. He has disappeared for all time, just as he did on those chill autumn nights with officers of the Metropolitan Police hot on his trail and the blood of his latest victim staining the cobblestones of some desolate alleyway.

He is not to be found among the 100 plus suspects put forward by various theorists. Each of those candidates can confidently be dismissed on grounds of simple logic, evidentiary conflict, or geographical impossibility. The suspect either does not match eyewitness accounts, lacks medical expertise, or has no knowledge of the terrain; he did not live in the East End or could not be placed there on the nights that Jack committed his dirty deeds. In some cases, Walter Sickert, for example, the suspect was many miles away on the nights of the murders (France, in this case).

So what do we know about Jack the Ripper, really? Based on various eyewitness reports, we are able to build up at least a partial description of the killer. The Ripper was said to be:

- A white male

- Average or below average height
- Strongly built
- Between 20 and 40 years of age.
- Respectably dressed

To that, we are able to add the professional opinions of the pathologists who examined the victims. They suggest that Jack:

- Was right-handed
- Had some medical expertise

We can also safely assume that he:

- Lived in the East End
- Had a regular job
- Was single or in a relationship where he was able to come and go as he pleased.
- Lived in private lodgings

There are also some useful clues offered by the profilers. Jack was probably:

- An introvert
- Someone who used prostitutes for sex and may have contracted a venereal disease as a result

- May have worked as a butcher, hospital worker, or mortician's assistant

- Probably already had a police record before he embarked on his campaign of terror.

And then there is the general data about serial killers gleaned by the FBI's Behavioral Science Unit from dozens of cases. They tell us that serial killers are most often:

- White males in their twenties and thirties
- Usually quite smart
- Underachievers who do poorly at school and end up in unskilled employment
- From broken homes with an absent or weak father and a domineering mother
- Physically, psychologically and/or sexually abused in childhood
- Bedwetters, fire starters, and animal abusers as children
- Hostile towards male authority figures and women
- Manifest psychological problems at an early age
- Have a general hatred towards humanity, including themselves
- Display an interest in sex at an unnaturally young age

Not a lot of tangible detail to go on, is it? As a writer, as a student of the case, as a reader who is fascinated by it, I am left wanting more. Like the authors who have come before me, like John Douglas and David Canter, I am left frustrated by the gaps in available data. Who was Jack really? What motivated him to carry out his frightful crimes? Why did he suddenly stop when at the height of his fury?

In the next section, I will attempt to answer some of these questions. I should stress that these answers, by necessity, require a great deal of speculation. However, these suppositions are in all cases based on verifiable facts from the case files, on what we know about psychopathy in general, and what we know specifically about the development and behavioral patterns of serial killers.

# Jack the Ripper Unmasked

*Key Questions About the Ripper Answered*

## What was Jack's childhood like?

We don't know where Jack was born or when. However, given the date of the murders and his likely age when he committed them, his probable date of birth was somewhere around the mid-1850s to early 1860s. As to his place of birth, it is possible that he was born and raised in the East End but just as likely that he was a foreigner, although most experts agree that he'd have lived in East London for at least a few years before the murders started.

It is unlikely that Jack was an only child since single child families were almost unheard of in those days. It is, however, possible (even probable) that some of his siblings died in childhood, as was common during that era. If Jack did grow up with siblings, he formed no close bonds with them.

It is probable that Jack's father was either absent or else entirely subjugated by Jack's domineering mother. I would suggest the latter since this would account for Jack's learned animosity towards women. Not that he necessarily hated his mother. I propose that the relationship was more love/hate in nature. We see examples of this in other serial killer cases. Seldom is their outright animosity between parent and child. More often, the child is desperate for parental approval but his efforts are thwarted by indifference.

In Jack's case, I submit that he was close to his father and was left bewildered by the way his father was treated by his mother. Early in life, he'd have formed the impression that women held the power to hurt and humiliate men. This would have clashed with his natural male drive for dominance. This conflicted mother/son relationship is present in the backgrounds of many serial killers - Ed Kemper, Joseph Kallinger, Bobby Joe Long, and Henry Lee Lucas, to name but a few.

Adding to Jack's perplexity would have been other aspects of his mother's behavior. She'd have been a heavy drinker, perhaps promiscuous and not afraid of flaunting her lovers in front of her husband. Perhaps she even worked part-time as a prostitute, as many East End women (including future Ripper victims) did. As Jack grew older, he'd have become ashamed of his mother's behavior. His playmates may have taunted him about it.

Jack's mother may not have been physically abusive to him in general terms. I favor the theory that she wasn't. The exception would have been in response to his bedwetting. I have little doubt that Jack was a bed wetter. Traumatized children often are. Soiled bed linen would have earned him physical punishment at the hands of his mother. She may also have inflicted psychological abuse, perhaps hanging out the stained bed sheet where his friends could see it, earning him further teasing and bullying. All of this would have caused him to withdraw further and further into himself.

As Jack grew older he'd have begun spending more and more time on his own. Solitary children often develop fantasy worlds and imaginary friends and Jack would have been no exception. His worlds, though, would have been nightmarish places filled with dreams of striking back against a system that he felt was stacked against him. How early might this have occurred? Probably earlier than you think. Another set upon child, Patrick Kearney, was dreaming about committing murder by the time he was eight. He'd later go on to claim over 30 lives as California's deadly "Trashbag Killer."

We need to pause here for a moment to consider an often controversial subject regarding the development of a serial killer. Are these monsters born bad or are they a product of their environment? Nature or nurture? Current thinking is that it is a combination of the two. The vast majority of serial killers are psychopaths and it is almost certain that Jack was one. Some of the characteristics of such a personality are a lack of empathy towards other people and a tendency to objectify them, a lack of conscience, and an appetite for risk and thrill seeking. All of these could easily be applied to Jack.

But not all psychopaths become serial killers, so there must have been something else in Jack's upbringing that veered him onto that path. The crimes of Jack the Ripper tell us exactly what that something was – fear-driven animosity towards women. That animosity can only have stemmed from his relationship with the woman closest to him - his mother.

What else is likely to have been true of Jack's childhood? I would wager that he was of above average intelligence although largely unschooled (as were most poor children in an era before compulsory education). There is a strong possibility that he indulged in anti-social acts such as arson, vandalism, and petty theft. This is common among fledgling serial killers and would have been his way of getting back at society. He may also have taken out his frustrations on smaller children or on animals. Perhaps he got his kicks by visiting the many slaughterhouses in the area to watch animals being violently put to death.

Jack, like many serial killers, probably had a precocious interest in sex but was at the same time terrified by the prospect of approaching a girl. John Douglas' profile suggests that his first sexual experience would have been with a prostitute. That rings true. The experience, I believe, would have left him feeling "dirty" and filled with self-loathing.

## What did Jack look like?

The common perception of Jack the Ripper is of a tall, well-dressed gentleman, traversing the mist-shrouded alleyways of Whitechapel, Gladstone bag in hand. Eyewitness accounts provide a somewhat different picture. At four of the five canonical murder sites (Chapman, Stride, Eddowes, and Kelly) there were sightings of a suspicious looking man. The descriptions are similar enough to suggest that this was Jack the Ripper.

The man is described as being of average to below average height, strongly built and in his mid-to-late twenties or early thirties. He is said to be well-dressed (shabby genteel, as one witness put it). He is wearing dark clothing and there is mention of a brown deerstalker hat by two witnesses. Some describe him as dark-skinned with a small black moustache, others describe the moustache as light-brown or "carroty." One witness mentions that his skin is blotchy. (John Douglas, incidentally, suggests that Jack might have had some minor "deformity" such as acne scarring.)

So what are we to make of these descriptions? Well, we should start by mentioning that eyewitness testimony is notoriously unreliable. Any detective will tell you this. However, when there is congruence between independent witnesses we need to pay attention. It is likely that the description of Jack as short and squat is true. It is likely that he was neatly dressed. (Douglas suggests he might have "dressed up" before going out on his hunts.)

But what of the differences in the descriptions provided by witnesses? Was Jack dark and "foreign-looking" or was he fair-haired with "blotchy skin"? It is interesting to note the stereotypes presented here. One describes a foreigner, the other, perhaps, an Englishman. Press speculation at the time of the Whitechapel Murders was that the killer was a foreigner and most probably a Jew. Might this have influenced the eyewitness descriptions? In all likelihood it did.

Of the witnesses who describe Jack as "foreign-looking," Elizabeth Long admitted that she saw him only from the back and George Hutchinson's testimony is highly suspicious and designed perhaps to insert himself into the investigation. Joseph Lawende and Israel

Schwartz got a better look at the Ripper. They describe him as fair with a small brown moustache. Schwartz's description is made all the more compelling because he saw the man engaged in a tussle with Liz Stride shortly before her dead body was discovered.

## Did Jack have medical training?

The issue of whether or not Jack had medical training was a contentious one at the time of the murders and remains contentious today. Most experts agree that Jack had at least some level of medical expertise although there are dissenters, most notably Dr. Thomas Bond, brought into the investigation specifically to evaluate whether Jack had any training in dissection. Dr. Bond concluded that Jack did not have "even the skill of a butcher or horse slaughter."

But perhaps there was an ulterior motive to Dr. Bond's denials, perhaps he was defending the honor of his profession. It should be remembered that the Ripper killed his victims in almost complete darkness. Then, working quickly, with the ever-present threat of discovery, he harvested hard-to-reach organs while leaving surrounding tissue intact. This points almost certainly to a man with skill and experience in wielding his knife. I would go further and say that Jack was not a butcher or horse slaughter but someone with some form of medical knowledge. I doubt that Jack was a doctor, since the police must have known about all physicians in the area and would surely have checked up on them.

John Douglas has suggested that perhaps Jack was a hospital worker, and I believe that to be a possibility. Maybe he was able to observe the surgeons at work or perhaps he was even present at anatomy classes (Whitechapel's London Hospital was a teaching institution).

We shall never know for certain. What is clear though is that Jack did not just hack at his victims with no purpose in mind. He knew what he wanted and he knew how to go about getting it.

**Why did he hate prostitutes?**

It is not necessarily true that Jack the Ripper hated prostitutes. His animosity, most likely, was directed at women in general. Prostitutes just happened to be easy targets, as respectable women would not have been found walking the streets unaccompanied late at night, and could not easily be lured to isolated spots by a complete stranger. Prostitutes were merely targets of convenience, as they have been for countless serial killers since.

I would also suggest that Jack's murders were not so much driven by hatred as by macabre curiosity. A hate-filled killer would have sought to inflict maximum suffering, with postmortem mutilations delivered mainly to the sex organs. Jack's murders seem altogether more calculated. The victims are incapacitated swiftly by strangulation. Then they are quickly dispatched by a couple of slashes to the throat. There is no inclination to inflict pain. His interest is primarily in the dead body.

Yet with the corpse under his control, he does not sexually violate her or attack the genitals. He guts the victim and removes specific organs – the uterus, the kidneys, the heart. To what purpose we shall never know but the purpose of the murder seems to be something other than outright rage. Jack was a necrophile rather than a sadist.

## What motivated him to kill?

Despite countless studies and hundreds of hours of interviews with captured serial killers, nobody knows what truly drives them. Each killer is unique, their motives ruled by compulsions we are not yet able to fully comprehend. Having said that, we are able to draw some conclusions from a forensic analysis of the Whitechapel murders themselves.

Brutal though they were, the crimes were not executed thoughtlessly. They were calculated to achieve a specific goal that only their perpetrator understood. That goal would have had its origins in Jack's fantasy world, developed over many years. He'd have committed murder many times in his mind before he killed his first victim.

But what might have driven him? His conflicted feelings towards woman that had its origins in his ambiguous relationship with his mother; his sexual frustration due to his shortcomings with the opposite sex; his ingrained fear of women grating up against his testosterone fueled instincts to dominate them; his sexual encounters with prostitutes, and the disgust he felt afterwards;

perhaps something more tangible, like a sexually transmitted disease due to one of those encounters. It might have been any or all of the above. One thing is certain, though. There must have been some tipping point.

How did Jack the Ripper go from a misogynistic fantasist to a wholesale slaughterer of woman? If other serial killers provide a template, then it was likely an accident.

Except that "accident" is perhaps not the correct word. What can be seen in many serial killer cases, is that the first murder is unplanned. It occurs when the killer is put into a stressful situation and responds to it. Jeffrey Dahmer committed his first murder after he brought a hitchhiker home and then decided he didn't want the man to leave. Denis Neilsen committed his first under remarkably similar circumstances. Joel Rifkin committed the first of his 17 prostitute murders because the woman angered him by insisting that he take her to buy drugs. Ted Bundy followed a young woman home with the intention of peeking into her apartment and ended up battering her as she slept. That victim survived but shortly thereafter Bundy set out to kill another woman and did just that.

It is my belief that Jack followed a similar path to murder. I find it unlikely that Polly Nichols, first of the Canonical Five, was his first victim. That murder seems too contrived, too planned. First murders tend to be messier, more spur of the moment.

One murder that might fit the bill as Jack's first was that of Martha Tabram, killed on August 7, 1888, some three weeks before the

August 31 slaying of Polly Nichols. Tabram was stabbed to death, suffering over 20 wounds. The murder took place in George Yard, less than a half-mile from where Nichols would be killed. Interestingly, Martha Tabram was killed on a landing in a tenement building, just a few feet from sleeping residents. And yet no one heard a sound, suggesting that she may have been choked before the killer turned his knife on her.

Was Martha Tabram Jack's first victim? I strongly suspect that she was. Perhaps he'd gone with her for a quick sexual encounter, a "four penny knee trembler" in the parlance of the day. But things got out of hand and he ended up throttling her and then stabbing her to death.

Killing is addictive to the serial killer. Jack would have relived the murder over and over in his mind. He'd have read the reports in the papers, and listened to the whispered conversations about the horrific crime. It would have left him feeling smug and self-satisfied. After all these years of being a nobody, of being society's punching bag, he'd struck back. And look at the effect he'd caused! People were quaking in fear and it was all because of him.

The afterglow of the murder would eventually have begun to fade, however, just as the compulsion to kill again was beginning to grow. He'd have planned this one more thoroughly. Martha Tabram had been killed with a small pen knife that he'd been carrying with him at the time. For what he now had in mind, he needed a longer and sharper blade. He would also have developed the idea of dressing up in his best suit. Easier to attract a whore if she thought you might have money.

Within weeks of the Tabram murder, Jack hit the streets, hunting this time. He'd by now thought through a methodology. Strangulation to stifle any cries then a sharp blade drawn across the throat, being careful to avoid the spurt of arterial blood. His hunts most likely started in one of the many taverns dotting the area. This served two purposes. Taverns were where whores gathered and it was easy to follow them once they hit the streets. He might also have needed a few drinks himself, to steady his nerves and lower his inhibitions.

## How many victims for the Ripper?

By today's standards, compared to the likes of Bundy and Dahmer and Chikatilo, Jack the Ripper is a relatively a run-of-the-mill serial killer. Most researchers credit him with five murders, the so-called "Canonical Five." Other experts discount canonical victim Elizabeth Stride. Still others include Stride and also Martha Tabram, killed on Tuesday, August 7, 1888, in the general vicinity of the other murders. Some say he continued killing after the last canonical murder (Mary Jane Kelly), claiming as many as nine kills.

My own opinion is that Jack was responsible for at least six murders, the "Canonical Five" plus Martha Tabram. We know that a man of very similar description was spotted near four of the murder scenes, sometimes in conversation with the victim (or in the case of Liz Stride, involved in an altercation). In the case of Polly Nichols, there was no eyewitness but the cuts to the victim's throat were so similar to the other victims that we can only assume that the same man was responsible.

Which leaves, Martha Tabram, discounted by some experts as a Ripper victim, included by others. The modus operandi in the Tabram murder was markedly different from the other five. Martha suffered multiple stab wounds inflicted with a small knife. Her throat was not slashed. Neither were there any postmortem mutilations. So how can a case be made for her as a Ripper victim?

To begin, we need to look at the murder of Polly Nichols, the first of the "Canonical Five." The murder, in that case, seems remarkably evolved, carried out swiftly and decisively with no hesitation and with a potential witness approaching the scene. First in series murders are seldom carried out with such efficiency, which means it is likely that Jack had killed before and the Tabram murder perfectly fits the bill. It was committed within a half mile of the others and was obviously carried out on the spur of the moment, possibly in the course of an altercation. However, one aspect of the crime is consistent with the others. Tabram was throttled to prevent her crying out. That, of course, would remain a signature of the Ripper murders.

**How did he choose his victims?**

In his 1988 profile of Jack the Ripper, Supervisory Special Agent John Douglas describes Jack in terms that are most often applied to disorganized serial killers (a loner, asocial, single, employed in unskilled labor). He also points out aspects of the Ripper crime scenes that suggest a disorganized offender (spontaneous attacks, victims chosen at random, bodies left where they fell). Douglas does not go as far as labeling Jack a disorganized serial killer with good reason. Such an assertion would be incorrect.

Many serial killers display both organized and disorganized characteristics and Jack is certainly one of them. There can be little doubt that he planned his attacks. Douglas suggests as much, proposing that Jack may have dressed up in his best suit in order to more easily attract his victims. And his killing method was precise, aimed at dispatching the victims with as little fuss as possible. These were not frenzied attacks. Jack likely derived very little pleasure from the actual kill. His real aim was to dispatch the victim as quickly as possible so that he could have his way with the corpse.

The actual victim type was unimportant. It is true that all of his victims, except Mary Kelly, were middle-aged, and all were prostitutes. However, they appear to have been chosen on the basis of availability, rather than preference. Prostitutes make easy victims. These were simply unfortunate enough to cross the Ripper's path while he was hunting.

## How did he kill his victims?

Much of Jack's M.O. has been covered elsewhere in this book. Essentially, he strangled his victim into submission, then lowered her to the ground, grasped her chin with his left hand and turned her head away from him. Positioning himself on the right side of the victim to prevent blood from spattering his clothes, he inflicted two deep cuts with his knife, using his right hand. These cuts ran left to right and were deep enough to sever the voice box and the main veins and arteries. The victim would have felt no pain.

With the victim now laying dead on the ground, the Ripper would have crouched down, spread her legs and lifted her skirts. Then, he'd have begun his mutilations, probably while straddling the body and pushing up the legs to shorten the distance to the abdomen. Given the time frames in which the murders are known to have been committed, he must have worked incredibly quickly. The only exception is the Mary Kelly murder, where he had time to indulge his most perverse fantasies.

There was never any indication that Jack had sex with his victims or masturbated over their corpses, as is often the case with sex killers. His enjoyment was derived from the horrendous postmortem wounds he inflicted. Sometimes he carried away a trophy, a section of the viscera, a kidney, the victim's uterus. The tidy excision of these organs led contemporary investigators to believe that he had some degree of anatomical knowledge.

**How was he able to evade the police?**

The East End during the 1800's was a labyrinth of alleyways, yards, and narrow streets, ill-lit and neigh on impossible to patrol effectively. As such, it was the perfect hunting ground for a serial killer, particularly one who knew the terrain well, as Jack must surely have.

Still, we should not underestimate the nerve and cunning it must have taken to stay one step ahead of the police. After the murder of Annie Chapman, the Met threw massive resources into Whitechapel and Spitalfields, placing hundreds of Bobbies on the streets. They even had some officers dressed up as prostitutes in the hope of luring the killer. Additionally, there were citizen's patrols, such as those organized by George Lusk's Mile End Vigilance Committee. It must have been difficult at the time to walk along any Whitechapel street at night and not run into one of these.

And yet, these measures were not sufficient to catch the Ripper, or even stop him killing. His bloodlust was such that despite the danger, he was back on the streets within weeks of killing Annie Chapman, claiming two victims in a single night.

The second of those murders (Catherine Eddowes) tells us a lot about the Ripper's personality. Eddowes was killed in Mitre Square, within the bounds of the City of London, an area not extensively patrolled at that time, a perfect escape route in other words. But Jack didn't take that option, he headed back into the East End, back towards the patrols, confident that he could outfox them. And outfox them, he did, although it was a close-run thing. His closest pursuers must have come across the strip of bloody apron moments after he dropped it. The Ripper, however, was gone.

It has been noted that psychopaths are risk seekers and this was certainly true of Jack. The thrill of the chase and the elation of evading his pursuers would have been all part of the game to him. In fact, it likely thrilled him more than the murder itself. The hunt, the mutilation of the corpse, and the subsequent escape – these were the things that excited him. The murder, carried out so quickly and so efficiently, was just a nasty bit of work he had to get out of the way.

## How would he have responded to news of his crimes?

Jack the Ripper would undoubtedly have followed the reportage of his deeds in the local papers. He would have delighted in the travails of the police and the obvious misinformation carried in the press. He would have relished the hushed conversations at work, and the bawdy conjecture in the taverns. Asked for an opinion, he'd have responded in measured tones, probably expressing his faith that the police would soon capture the "monster." He would likely have dropped a few subtle hints into the conversation, disguised as opinion.

How do we know this? We know because this is how serial killers behave. Some keep newspaper cuttings of their crimes, others hang out at bars frequented by cops, others seek to inject themselves into the investigation by claiming to be a witness, or by communicating with the authorities. It seems clear that they have an interest in how their deeds are perceived. Jack, of course, could not have avoided this. During those bloody three months, he was the only news in town.

It seems likely as well that Jack would have been questioned by the police during the course of their investigation. The police, after all, did door-to-door inquiries and Jack lived in the area. A visit from the police would have thrilled him, but he'd have given nothing away. Psychopaths have stunted emotional responses, one of the reasons why they are often able to pass polygraphs. Jack would have aroused no suspicion.

Would he have gone further, for example offering himself as an eyewitness? John Douglas thinks not, and I am inclined to agree with him. This, of course, rules out two men sometimes mentioned as Ripper suspects, Charles Cross (first on the scene at the Nichols murder) and George Hutchinson (who claimed to have seen the Ripper with Mary Kelly).

And what of the Ripper letters, how would Jack have responded to those? Assuming that he did not write the letters himself (and most experts believe that he did not), I believe that the letters would have annoyed Jack. He would not have liked someone else taking credit for his work. This is a behavior common in serial killers. We see them castigating court officials for understating their misdeeds, we see them confessing to crimes where there is no evidence to convict, some experts even believe that they deliberately slip up so that they can be caught and thus receive "credit" for their murders.

So Jack would not have liked someone else claiming his kills. He would also have been annoyed when the police named John Pizer (Leather Apron) as their key suspect.

One aspect of the Ripper letters that Jack would have enjoyed is the salutation "Jack the Ripper." It is quite common in serial murder cases, for the press or public to assign a nickname to an unknown killer. And, as epithets go, this one is perfect, at once terrifying and catchy. Jack, I believe, would have liked it.

## Why was there such an escalation of violence from one crime to the next?

Escalation in serial murder cases is the rule rather than the exception. There are a number of reasons for this. Firstly, these murders are fantasy fueled and fantasy very seldom matches up to reality. The killer has an idea about what he wants to do to the victim and, more importantly, how it will make him feel. However, when he commits the crime, he finds that the thrill falls somewhat short of expectation. With the next murder, he tries to rectify that, acting out in more extreme ways. But, yet again, he falls short, perpetuating the cycle.

Secondly, there is the issue of addiction. Serial murder has been called just that and, as any recovering addict will tell you, you need a progressively bigger hit, just to attain the same high. It is the same with serial killers. Many (like Bianchi and Buono, Bittaker and Norris, Donald Gaskins) have actually admitted to experimenting with different methods of murder and torture in order to get their kicks.

Thirdly, there is the issue of pent-up emotion. Serial killers are known to have a "cooling off" period between murders, ranging from days to years. During this time, they will relive their latest kill in their minds until the fantasy becomes inadequate to their needs and they are compelled to kill again. In Jack's case, this cooling off period was particularly short, and not entirely of his own making. In the periods immediately after each murder, he was forced to lay low, due to the increased police presence and his favored prey deserting the streets.

Jack the Ripper was clearly a man who harbored a great deal of anger and animosity. Murder and mutilation provided an outlet for these frustrations, and being prevented from acting out would have resulted in him becoming increasingly agitated. When he eventually was able to alleviate this, the result would have been explosive.

Thus, we see a clear escalation of violence in the Ripper case. The murders of Polly Nichols and Liz Stride can be disregarded since, on these two occasions, Jack was interrupted. As for the other three canonical murders – Chapman was eviscerated; Eddowes was eviscerated and there were also severe mutilations to her face.

And then, there was Mary Jane Kelly. In the earlier murders, Jack had mere minutes to carry out his mutilations. In this case, he had hours, and he used them to indulge his deepest, darkest fantasies. The extent of the terrible injuries inflicted on Kelly is documented elsewhere in this book. Suffice to say that this murder ranks among the most horrific in the annals of crime.

**Why did he stop?**

In order to answer the question of why, we must first determine when. There are two schools of thought. The first is that Mary Jane Kelly was the last of the Ripper's victims. The second is that Jack remained at large until at least 1891, claiming several more victims. I am firmly in the former camp. For one reason or another, all of the supposed later victims must be excluded from the series.

So if we conclude that the Ripper stopped killing after he murdered Mary Kelly, the question is why? John Douglas offers three suggestions – he came close to being arrested and thus decided to quit; he was arrested and incarcerated for an unrelated crime; he committed suicide. Douglas then immediately discounts the possibility of suicide and I am inclined to agree with him. Serial killers do not generally kill themselves while at large. The only cases I am aware of happened while the killer was in custody.

As for the idea that the killer might have stopped out of fear of capture, that just does not ring true in this case. The violence inflicted on Mary Kelly points to a person who was growing in his compulsion, not someone who would have been able to back down. Once the need began to grow again, the Ripper would have been back on the streets, hunting. And given his earlier pattern, that scenario would have occurred within weeks, rather than months.

Which leaves us with the theory of arrest on an unrelated crime. This is quite possible, of course. In recent years, we've seen a number of cold cases resolved where the perpetrator was found to already be behind bars. Was this the fate of Jack the Ripper? Did he die while incarcerated for something totally unrelated to the Whitechapel murders? Was he released sometime in the 1920s or 30s as an old man? Was he able to keep his dark secrets for all those years inside? Maybe. Possibly. We don't know.

Another variant of the imprisonment theory is that Jack was banged up in an insane asylum (some say he went mad after killing Mary Kelly). I find this version of events less plausible. If there is one thing we do know about Jack the Ripper, it is that he was not insane. A psychopath, yes, but not a psychotic. A madman would not have been able to talk a victim into a dark alley or maintain such a consistent M.O., or act so coolly under pressure. As for the ludicrous idea that the murder of Mary Kelly tipped him over the edge into insanity, the man was a psychopath, emotionally stunted, devoid of empathy. Killing and mutilating a woman would scarcely have quickened his pulse, let alone driven him mad.

There is one other possibility of what might have happened to Jack, one not considered by Douglas. He may have been killed or died of natural causes. I find this idea quite compelling. Average life expectancy in 1880's Britain was just 40 years. Disease was rife and medical care, especially among the poor, inadequate. Jack, who likely used prostitutes for sex, was at high risk of contracting an STD or other infectious disease. He also lived in a high crime area and being out on the streets late at night, he might well have become a victim of violence himself, a gang mugging perhaps. His habit of dressing as a gentleman might well have attracted criminals to him. Would that not have been an irony.

# Catch Me a Killer

*A Simple Investigative Strategy to Identify*

*the Ripper at Last*

We do not know the identity of Jack the Ripper, neither are we
ever likely to know. Jack has eluded us, disappeared into the mists
of time forever. And yet that doesn't stop us trying to unravel the
mystery. Perhaps there is some elusive scrap of information that
someone else has overlooked or misinterpreted, perhaps that
tenuous clue that finally unlocks the puzzle. After all, it's not as
though our knowledge of the Ripper has remained static. We know
a lot more now than we did, even ten years ago.

I can still remember my initial reactions when reading about the
case as an impressionable teenager. They invoked a vision of a tall,
aristocratic gentleman in a cloak and top hat, stalking the ghettos
with his implements of hell (as Albert Fish would have called
them) concealed within a Gladstone bag. Now we know different.
We know that Jack was no gentleman but a denizen of the East
End, like the poor women he preyed on. We know that he was not
tall and aristocratic, but short and stubby, not well-dressed but
playing at being well-dressed.

We know, too, a little bit about his likely character – a loner with
low self-esteem, unmarried and with strong feelings of animosity

towards women, a man in regular but unskilled employment, a night owl wandering the darkened streets, searching.

Other questions remain unanswered. Was he a doctor? Likely not. Did he have some form of medical expertise? It would be hard to imagine him committing the crimes without it. Why did he kill, why did he stop? We simply don't know.

Is there any light at the end of the tunnel, any field of investigation that might offer an answer? Perhaps. The profile compiled by John Douglas suggests that Jack most likely had a police record, perhaps for rape or assault, before he escalated to murder. Douglas also suggests that the Ripper might have been a hospital worker, employed at the London Hospital in Whitechapel. Furthermore, we have drawn the conclusion that the Ripper either died or was imprisoned shortly after the Kelly murder. If we check the records for candidates meeting all three of those criteria we will have significantly narrowed the field.

And we can hone in even further than that. A recent examination of the evidence using a technique called "geographical profiling" has revealed the likely location of Jack the Ripper's residence. The study was carried out by Dr. Kim Rossmo, a former Canadian police officer who has used the method to track down several high profile criminals. It utilizes a computer algorithm, drawing input from the locations of the crimes and the killer's likely movements.

The results of this study suggest that the Ripper most likely lived on Flower and Dean Street, a small thoroughfare that ran off Brick Lane, in close proximity to the Ten Bells pub. The street, unfortunately, no longer exists. It was bombed into oblivion during the London blitz. Rossmo, however, is certain that Jack lived there, or at least spent a significant amount of time there.

So now we have four inputs to consider. Surely that must narrow our list to a handful of suspects, perhaps just one, perhaps Jack the Ripper himself?

Unfortunately, it is not that simple. Police archives from the era are far from complete, while residency records are non-existent and records of employment are patchy. It's another dead end. Despite the millions of research hours and the copious volumes produced on the case, Jack remains as elusive as ever, frustrating all of our efforts to unmask him.

As a student of the case for many years (I hesitate to use the term Ripperologist) I have walked this path and I know how maddening it can be. The answers seem so close and yet so far away, so tenuous. If you are similarly frustrated, then the only thing I can offer is to relax and embrace the mystery.

Think about it. Had Jack been caught in the days after he brutalized Mary Kelly, had George Hutchinson encountered him on the street and been able to point him out to a police officer, where would we be now? Certainly not pondering the greatest enigma in criminal history.

*For more True Crime books by Robert Keller please visit*

*http://bit.ly/kellerbooks*

52076820R00094

Made in the USA
San Bernardino, CA
10 August 2017